Heavenly Humor
for the Woman's Soul

Heavenly Humor
for the Woman's Soul

BARBOUR
PUBLISHING

ISBN 978-1-60260-030-0

Published by Barbour Publishing, Inc., P.O. Box 719, Uhrichsville, Ohio 44683
www.barbourbooks.com

Our mission is to publish and distribute inspirational products offering exceptional value and biblical encouragement to the masses.

Member of the
Evangelical Christian
Publishers Association

Printed in the United States of America.

Contents

Introduction

Tina Krause

Laughter is God's medicine, the most beautiful therapy God ever gave humanity.
ANONYMOUS

The washing machine overflows, your toddler comes down with the chicken pox, the septic system fails, and you still have a casserole to prepare and tables to decorate for the big family reunion you promised to host in your home the next day.

It's tough to smile at times like these. Most of us would rather stay in bed, pull the sheets over our heads, and refuse to budge until things got better. Yet when life's irritants bug us more than a swarm of pesky mosquitoes and troubles spread faster than cold germs, laughter is what we need the most.

The physiological benefits of laughter have been tested from the boardroom to the hospital room. Some corporations send their CEOs to seminars on humor because they have discovered a correlation between having a sense of humor and making sound business decisions. Scientists suggest that laughter reduces stress levels, lowers blood pressure, boosts the immune system, and actually releases endorphins that diminish physical pain!

Humor is heart therapy. In fact, one doctor called laughter "internal jogging," claiming that laughing one hundred times a day works the heart as much as exercising for ten minutes on a rowing machine or fifteen minutes on an exercise bike. And what woman wouldn't rather laugh than sweat?

But long before medical science heralded the benefits of laughter, God said: "A cheerful heart is good medicine" (Proverbs 17:22); "A happy heart makes the face cheerful" (Proverbs 15:13); and, "A cheerful look brings joy to the heart, and good news gives health to the bones" (Proverbs 15:30). God created laughter to lift our spirits, lighten our loads, heal our bodies, and provide a temporary reprieve from our chaotic lives.

Despite your station in life and whatever mishaps, mayhem, or maladies you face today, it is my prayer that this book will—in some small way—provide you with a temporary relief from your pain, a short reprieve from your chaos, and renewed hope for a better day ahead.

So join me. Curl up in a cozy chair, indulge yourself in a warm cup of tea, and begin to bolster your spirit with some heavenly humor.

Home

Not Just Monkeying Around

Debora M. Coty

"Therefore do not worry about tomorrow. . . .
Each day has enough trouble of its own."
MATTHEW 6:34

I grinned at the newspaper clipping. "Wild Chimps Observed Making Spears for Hunting"* only confirmed what I'd suspected all along: Women are the real innovators.

The article highlighted female chimpanzees in Senegal fabricating weapons in a multistep process. "The landmark observation also supports the long-debated proposition that females—the main makers and users of spears among the Senegalese chimps—tend to be the innovators and creative problem solvers in primate culture."

"Aha!" I waved the telltale article beneath my husband's nose. "That's why 'Necessity is the *mother* of invention,' not the father!"

Chuck was quick to point out a paragraph describing the lady chimps repeatedly stabbing their prey: "'It was really alarming how forceful it was,' said lead researcher Jill D. Pruetz of Iowa State University, adding that it reminded her of the murderous shower scene in the Alfred Hitchcock movie *Psycho*. 'It was kind of scary.'"

Recalling my own psycho-frenzied behavior on numerous occasions, I felt an odd kinship with those hairy gals. They were probably married with children. A recent *Psycho* moment came to mind.

The previous Friday, I'd invited my daughter, her fiancé, and future in-laws for dinner. With an hour to go, I'd allowed precisely enough time in my tight schedule to zip-clean my house and fix dessert. I had just set out éclair pie fixings and evacuated the dinette chairs and throw rugs to mop the kitchen when Chuck's frantic cry for help resounded. Naturally, he'd picked that moment to fix the leaky tub faucet and water was shooting all over the bathroom.

Using a skillet lid as a shield, I fended off the water blast to get close enough to divert the geyser while Chuck dashed outside to shut off the water to the house. By that time, whitecaps dotted Lake Coty.

Every towel in the house was gathered to sop up the mess when the doorbell rang. The cable guy had arrived to repair the order we'd submitted five days before. He was followed inside by an irate neighbor screaming about her neglected repair request, and I retreated to the kitchen where my whipped topping had been reduced to the consistency of clabbered cream.

Layering graham crackers and now-unwhipped cream and pudding in a large dish, I was nearly finished when I happened to pop a broken cracker in my mouth. *EWWWW! Rancid!* What to do? No time for the store!

The doorbell chimed again. I had to answer. Chuck was

still swimming in Lake Coty.

I sprinted back to the kitchen and scraped pudding from fifty-eight nasty crackers. I never knew old graham crackers taste like the stuff you scrape off your shoe after tipping cows.

Plundering through my cabinets, I found another box. Shooting a prayer heavenward, I taste-tested a cracker. *Thank you, Lord!* I respread the rescued pudding and topped it with fudge sauce. No one need ever know.

While I dragged the overflowing trash can outside, Chuck resurfaced and helpfully replaced the kitchen chairs and rugs, assuming I'd already mopped.

I heaved them back into the living room and ran to squeegee the flooded bathroom. I returned to find that Chuck had again replaced the chairs and rugs on the dirty kitchen floor. Or maybe they got homesick and waddled back themselves.

At that moment, our guests arrived.

In these laugh-or-cry situations, thanks, Lord, for helping Your innovators choose to laugh!

*Tampa Tribune article, 2/23/07

Laundry

Toni Sortor

*There is a time for everything, and a season
for every activity under heaven.*
ECCLESIASTES 3:1

In our house, a piece of laundry takes about four days from start to finish. The first day it's run through the washer and dryer. The second, it sits in the dryer developing the proper number of wrinkles. The third day I reheat and fold it. The fourth day it's put away. That's assuming I haven't run out of something vital or created a roadblock by washing more than one load a day, in which case folded laundry piles up, and the cats sleep on it, requiring a second run through the washer and dryer.

I don't normally procrastinate in life's little chores. Papers never pile up on my desk. I have a mental to-do list and enjoy working my way through it, but somehow laundry always sinks to the bottom of my list. We adapt. I can wear a pair of jeans for two days, if necessary. My husband has discovered he can wear a bathing suit under his business suit when all else fails, since he would not think of buying a week's worth of anything at once.

Things are not going to change, laundry-wise. Now that

the kids are gone, so is my motivation. Now doing laundry frees up time to read a book, visit the grandchildren, go fishing, or even take a nap. I love laundry simply because I can always put it off without guilt for another day.

WORDS A WOMAN WILL NEVER SAY

"What a rotten day. This new dress makes me look ten pounds slimmer, my husband cleaned the house while I was at work, and the kids threatened to do their own laundry if I refused to put my feet up and relax all evening. Now I ask you, how much more can a woman take?"

Squirrelly Girly

Rachel St. John-Gilbert

*For everything in the world—the cravings of sinful man,
the lust of his eyes and the boasting of what he has and does—
comes not from the Father but from the world.*
1 JOHN 2:16

Most women have a hard time keeping a pristine home unless they hire help to keep it that way. I often wonder if we worry too much about what others will think—we are so often our own harshest critics. Perhaps we would be a little easier on ourselves if we heard a different view.

My writing friend Susan lives in the country with her husband and three sons. Her boys hunt in the fields and fish in the creeks, so Susan doesn't have them underfoot too often. Even so, with her writing projects, speaking engagements, and travel schedule, her house usually leans more toward Rat's Nest than Pristine. In other words, if cleanliness is next to godliness, Susan hasn't got a prayer.

However, if lovability is next to godliness, Susan is a saint. Most of her friends, including me, love it that Susan's house is usually in a state of disarray. There's something freeing about never worrying about spilling coffee on—well, anything. Equally nice is the fact that we aren't tempted to compare our homes with hers and feel discouraged or jealous. We can prop up our feet and let the good times roll! Susan usually has us rolling right away with her storytelling skills. She is a walking treasure trove of "truth is stranger than fiction" funny stories. And the last one was a doozey:

"I'd been to a Bible study," she began, "and afterward my car wouldn't start. Well, Claire Smith—a new gal in town—offered to take me home.

" 'I'd love to see your house.' Claire beamed. 'You know—where you write, how you manage with children.' I could feel the panic rising, remembering how I'd left my house that morning.

"At the front door I tried to prepare her.

" 'It might be a little messy. . . ,' I said. Reaching the kitchen counter, I cleared away cereal bowls and wiped up warm sticky milk as fast and inconspicuously as I could. Claire was still all smiles and seemed unmoved by the mess. 'Let me see what I have in the fridge here,' I rambled. 'I think I have some cheese and grapes we could snack on while we visit. We'll sit out on the back porch. . . .'

"My thought was to get Claire out of the house as quickly as possible, but when I opened the fridge, I gasped and shut the door in record time. I've encountered many interesting things in my refrigerator, but this time, even I was shocked.

Staring me in the face was the carcass of a rabbit and the pelt of a squirrel. Obviously my sons had been big-game hunting.

"I took Claire gently by the arm and ushered her to the back porch.

" 'Tell you what,' I suggested. 'Why don't you sit here in the porch swing while I fix the tray?'

"An hour later, we were fast friends, and I told her the truth about what was in the fridge. She laughed till she cried. Girls, Claire's gonna fit in just fine!"

Susan finished her saga with this jewel. "Thank y'all so much for taking me just as I am—without one plea. Except, maybe, insanity."

"You know we wouldn't have you any other way!" I insisted. "Remember, *some* people say a clean house is a sign of a sick mind."

What is it about a "be yourself" kind of friend that is so irresistible? Maybe it reminds us of what unconditional love feels like. To be able to completely relax in someone's presence and home is a gift; and we can thank God for those who give us that relational luxury. We can even take mental notes and learn how to do the same for others when they come to our place. Maybe Susan can loan us some squirrel pelts to get us started.

House Cleaning

Toni Sortor

For he will deliver the needy who cry out,
the afflicted who have no one to help.
PSALM 72:12

I discovered long ago that I was not good at cleaning. Some people actually enjoyed it, but I found it as rewarding as having teeth pulled. The problem is, you are never done with it, never satisfied that you captured every last dust bunny or swept away every cookie crumb. Even if you did, more would begin to accumulate before you put away the mop. Cleaning has a certain built-in futility.

But I did it for a good twenty years as the children grew up, and nobody ever caught a horrible disease from the cobwebs I knew I missed. When I went back to work and collected my first pitiful paycheck, it finally dawned on me that I could pay other people to clean my house. My mother had never had help, even though she worked all her life, but she was a better woman than I am, or at least less compulsive.

Ever since then I've had a crew of people who appear every week and accomplish more in one hour than I could by cleaning every spare second of my day. I still have to do some cleaning, but the burden is off my back. Help arrives every

Wednesday afternoon, regular as clockwork, and I don't go looking for trouble in corners or anywhere else. To me this is the abundant life in spades.

Marriage

Running on Empty

Debora M. Coty

Should your springs overflow in the streets,
your streams of water in the public squares?
PROVERBS 5:16

While rereading Dr. Gary Chapman's *The Five Love Languages,* the importance of actually speaking the language of the one with whom we're trying to communicate was demonstrated to me in a most memorable way.

My husband and I were visiting picturesque Innsbruck, Austria, on our first trip abroad. By the third day, the cuisine disagreed with my delicate internal fortitude. I began to feel the effects of the middle *Rhea* sister of that infamous trio, Pyor*Rhea*, Diar*Rhea*, and Gonor*Rhea.* Yep, I was assaulted by the Innsbruck trots.

Frantically searching for the Bavarian equivalent of Walgreens, I discovered a sign down the street from our hotel bearing a long German word reminiscent of "apothecary," the old-fashioned term for drugstore.

Aha! I'll just run in there and find something that looks like Immodium.

So I shuffled into the shop, knees together and rear cheeks clinched, to find a wall-to-wall glass counter behind which were stored all the goods. Three stern-faced clerks were taking orders. Uh-oh. I knew zero German.

It's okay, I thought, *I hear everyone in Europe knows English. No big deal.*

"Hello." I flashed a smile. "Do you speak English?"

"*Sprechen sie Deutsch,*" the clerk replied tersely.

Oh dear. "Does anyone here speak English?" I gestured toward the other employees.

"Sprechen sie Deutsch," she stated firmly, as if to imply, "You dope, where do you think you are, Disneyland?"

Think, Debbie. . .I know! I've always been good at charades. I'll act it out!

Glancing at the other now-gawking customers, I leaned over the counter and whispered, "I" (pointed to my chest)—"need" (pointed to knee)—"medicine" (mimed popping pills into my mouth)—"for" (held up four fingers)—um, um. . . "diarrhea" (gestured a river flowing deep and wide).

"EH?"

At that moment, a dozen Japanese tourists crowded into the tiny shop, packing us in like a box of toothpicks. The clerk stared at me, waiting. I considered giving up, but that Rhea sister wasn't just knocking on my door, she was pounding with both fists.

Deep breath. *Try again.* "I" (pointed to my chest)—"have" (fist in other hand)—"the runs" (high-kneed running in place with sphincter muscles kicking into high gear).

The customers behind me tittered. The clerk shook her head and jabbered loudly to her cohort as my dignity melted into a puddle on the floor. I was deathly afraid that something very nasty was about to follow.

A Japanese woman from the back of the crowd made her way to my side. She bowed. I bowed back. Then, bless her compassionate heart, she uttered the three most beautiful words I'd ever heard: "Please. . .me. . .help?"

"Oh yes! *Sí! Oui!* Toshiba! Kawasaki!" (I don't speak Japanese either.)

Trilingual, she translated my dilemma to the clerk in German, ending her monologue with, "English. . .di–ree–ah."

"Ah, di–ree–ah," the clerk echoed, heading for the supply shelves. She suddenly turned and chattered to my interpreter, who translated with accompanying gestures. "You. . .small di–ree–ah (fingers one inch apart), or BIG di–ree–ah (hands spanning four feet)?"

With face flaming, I had no choice but to reply with the appropriate in-between gesture, "Medium di–ree–ah."

Not the makings of a fond vacation memory perhaps, but a very effective reminder that if I don't put forth effort to speak the love language my spouse understands, I might as well be speaking a foreign language.

Complex by Design

Helen Widger Middlebrooke

*Husbands, love your wives, even as Christ also loved the church,
and gave himself for it.*
EPHESIANS 5:25 KJV

A sportswriter I know once wrote a column explaining how simple men are.

Inspired by this, I wanted to write an essay explaining how simple women are.

But I couldn't. Because women are not simple.

Just ask Mike. After nineteen years, he still hasn't figured me out.

Say, for example, he comes home to find me crying. To his simple cause-and-effect mind, something must have caused the crying, so he reacts accordingly:

"What's wrong?"

"Nothinggggg," I'll wail.

"Then why are you crying?"

"I don't knowwwwww."

"Why don't you stop?"

"Because I feel like crying!"

He'll walk away shaking his head, muttering.

I also make him mutter at vacation time. While he

leisurely packs his one suitcase, I clean the house, wash every piece of dirty laundry, pack for at least five kids and myself, and make sure all of them are in clean underwear (in case we have an accident).

Then I stuff my tote bag with unread magazines and newsletters, receipts, and a few notebooks. The first hundred miles, I post receipts and tally food expenditures.

"Ah," he'll say, "we're on vacation."

That's what he thinks. I'm still trying to get caught up and organized so I can relax. My house and family are extensions of me—and if they're not in order, I'm not in order.

And then there are times when I'm stressed out over a problem:

"I've got to take two to piano lessons from 2:00 to 3:00, get two at school at 3:00 and be downtown for an appointment by 3:15. This is crazy!"

"So why don't you have the boys walk home?" he'll say calmly.

Idiot! I knew that. I didn't want him to solve my problem. I just wanted him to feel my pain.

Sometimes I wish I could be less complicated, but it's not in my nature.

And that's not my fault. We women have been complicated since creation.

God made Adam simply, from "the dust of the earth." But He made Eve from Adam's rib, a more complicated process.

We are wonderfully, annoyingly complex by design.

We weren't meant to be figured out. We were meant to be loved.

It's as simple as that.

I know I annoy him, sometimes, Father, because I look at life so differently. Give him the wisdom to understand me and the patience to endure.

Love Match

Debora M. Coty

Reckless words pierce like a sword,
but the tongue of the wise brings healing.
PROVERBS 12:18

As a tennis addict, it occurred to me that tennis strokes are a lot like the verbal strokes we use when communicating with our spouses. Rallying between partners is much the same, whether the weapon of choice is an oversized racket or an overly reckless tongue.

Ideally, our conversations should start out with a serve and return—relaying the ball back and forth in a loving, peaceable manner.

She: "How was work today, dear?" (Kiss)

He: "Fine, although the boss moved my project deadline up two weeks because of his trip to Austria. But enough about me; how was your day, sug-ums? (Hands her flowers) Mmm, I smell dinner! You look a little tired—can I give you a shoulder massage?"

She: "That would be lovely, pookie, thanks for asking. Oh, there were a few appliance glitches and the children—bless their little hearts—needed a bit of maternal guidance, but the sky was blue, the larks were singing, and I was glad to be alive!"

Sometimes one partner rushes the net and goes for the overhead smash, the real conversation killer:

She: "How was work today, dear?" (Kiss is cut off in midair)

He: "Terrible. Rotten. Heinous. Zero on a scale of one to ten. (Flings flowers around) How in thunder am I supposed to get my project finished two weeks early? What is that disgusting smell—did something die in here? (Fans nose with flowers) That stupid boss of mine—he's almost as lame-brained as your mother!

Or both players rush the net and get into a quick volley exchange:

He: "What a horrible day!"

She: "Ha! You think yours was bad?"

He: "Ye-ah! My imbecile boss dumped tons of extra work on me so he can waltz off to Europe—"

She: "Listen, bub, you don't have a clue! First Tiffany tried to wash her tennis bag with the racquet still inside and the washing machine overflowed and drowned the cat; then the microwave exploded because Junior tried to dry the phone after he dropped it in the toilet."

He: "Do you mind? I'm trying to tell you about *my* day!"

She: "No, I don't mind a bit. And then *your* son decided one fire wasn't enough so he—"

He: "*My* son? So now he's *my* son?" (Gestures wildly with flowers)

She: "Yes, *your* son!" (Grabs flowers and hits him over the head)

He: "You're the one who wanted another kid!"

She: "But it was your chromosome that made it a boy!"

Occasionally, an ace is served:

He enters and opens his mouth to speak.

She: "Ohhhhh no! Don't you dare get started on your lousy stinking day! I don't even want to hear it after the miserable day I've had!"

He: "But. . ."

She: "NO, I can't hear you. . .LALALALALALALA!" (Hands over ears)

Remember, girls, we don't have to win every love match. God is more concerned with the comfort and healing our words bring than the aces we score. After all, we're on the same team as our partners, and we want to make it to the finals!

WORDS A WOMAN WILL NEVER SAY

"Excuse me, dear, but must we always talk about our feelings?"

Dancing in the Frozen-Food Aisle

Dena Dyer

You have turned my sorrow into joyful dancing.
No longer am I sad and wearing sackcloth.
PSALM 30:11 CEV

On my mother's side, I come from a long line of "creatives." Which is a nice way of saying our family is a little whacked-out.

My great-grandfather wrote tons of unpublished short stories, some of which I have. His daughter, Nanaw, was an artist and writer, as well as an art teacher. Her husband, Dadaw, was an amateur inventor and held several patents before he died. And my mother is a talented decorator and has published a few stories of her own.

I love my nontypical bloodline. But I have noticed that sometimes the craziness inherent in creative people comes at the expense of their family members' comfort.

For instance, Nanaw and Dadaw used to dance to the Muzak in the grocery store, much to my mother's chagrin. While they waltzed around the frozen food, she hid behind the stacks of canned goods, praying no one would see her. Their defense? "We can't let this good music go to waste!"

I know I've been an embarrassment—and a frustration—

to my darling hubby at times. (I will be to my son, too, as soon as he's old enough to realize I'm not "normal.") Even though my husband is a professional entertainer, he tends to keep his creativity at work. I, on the other hand, love to decorate and redecorate. In fact, Carey never knows when he'll come home to a totally different house than the one he left that morning!

He loves to tell people about my goofs, too—like the afternoon I decided our office wall could use some inspirational art. Instead of taking the time to find a stencil, I proceeded to freehand on the wall, with a Magic Marker, a "feel-good" quote about writing. (Hey, it looked oh-so-easy and oh-so-lovely when Lynette Jennings did it on HGTV.)

My version looked horrible, although I did cover it up nicely with a quilt. However, Carey often pulls up the blanket to show visitors the "artwork" on the office wall, as if to say, "Look what I put up with!"

To be fair, Carey also brags on me incessantly and says my wacky side keeps our marriage fun and interesting. Recently, when I told him I had always wanted to go to circus camp and learn the trapeze, his mouth dropped open and he shook his head. "We've been married ten years, and you just now tell me this?" he asked. "Honey, I love you. . .but I'll never understand you."

At least he'll never get bored!

In fact, he encouraged me to write about my grandparents dancing in the aisles. "What a great story!" he said. "You have to write that down."

And I do love the mental picture of Nanaw and Dadaw shunning convention and kicking up their heels in the middle of "Thrift-Mart," especially since I never really knew my grandfather. I know he suffered from depression, and I know he basically worried himself to death at a relatively young age.

But somehow, in the grocery store, my grandmother's influence over him—or his own sense of absurdity—helped him let go of his worries and embrace life.

Maybe the next time I go shopping, I'll do the same.

Sizzling After Sixty

Rachel St. John-Gilbert

Therefore shall a man leave his father and his mother,
and shall cleave unto his wife: and they shall be one flesh.
GENESIS 2:24 KJV

As I enter my forties and notice more wrinkles and bulges from head to toe, I have become more curious about the "birds and bees" in a person's advancing years. The other day I saw a book titled *Sex After Sixty*. Glancing around to make sure my pastor wasn't in the bookstore, I casually picked it up and flipped through the pages. The contents shocked me. Every page was filled with nothing but. . .white space.

A few days later, I dropped by my mom's house. When I told her about falling for the book, she laughed.

"Don't you believe it!" she assured me. "There's plenty of adventure to fill that book, for the *fun* of it, if nothing else. I remember the card your dad received from a buddy for his sixtieth birthday. The front pointed out that at our age, sex isn't exactly the Fourth of July. Inside the card, it said at our age sex is more like Thanksgiving."

Mom continued, "To adjust to the changes that come along with the wrinkles and pounds"—*Now we're getting somewhere*, I thought—"you gotta learn to laugh. One winter's night, my Sweet Thang hopped into bed before I did. When I joined him, I squealed with ecstatic gratitude. He had remembered to turn on my side of the electric blanket!"

Well, now I was laughing, but feeling a smidgen sorry for the old folks when Mom explained, "Have you ever heard the lines from Robert Browning's poem? 'Grow old along with me! The best is yet to be'?"

"Sure," I said, nodding. "But the motto for most of my generation is more like 'Grow to midlife with me, then let's divorce.'"

Mom chuckled and said, "Yes, I'm not sure what to make of your generation! But I wouldn't trade any part of our marriage of fifty years for the part we're in right now—not even the years when I was in my prime and you and your siblings made our rendezvous a lot more challenging!

"Then came our Empty Nest phase. For most couples, if things go as planned, the kids all grow up and go away, and Mom and Dad are alone again. By this time, the soil of understanding, affection, and experience has been tilled. The hormones are still pumping well, and Cupid finds he has a couple of pros to work with.

"But as time goes by, Aunt Minnie Paws drops in to visit Mom about the same time Dad finds that his Don-Juan Readiness can't always be counted on. Add to that a natural drop in energy levels, and you may well have to take a nap before enjoying a nighttime romance."

"So much for spontaneity!" I quipped.

"Well, sometimes, yes, spontaneity goes out the window.

However, when love has been growing as it should, Mom and Dad find that they *like* each other so much more than when they were first married. By this time, deep affection has usually replaced less reliable passion. Tender understanding of the physical changes each has experienced can lead over-sixty couples to explore new ways of expressing the joy of coming together.

"Next day, Don Juan struts off to the golf course with a spring in his step and a glint in his eye. Mom can hardly remember how it feels to be sixty-five, now that she's sixteen again."

Pausing for breath, Mom winked at me and advised, "Take your vitamins—there's definitely sex after sixty! Rarely do the pages of a good, long marriage go blank until well past that age."

In our culture of "instant" everything—from microwave meals to spray-on suntans, we can lose sight of the concept that many things get better with time. Wine and cheese for example. Kids, too (although some of you will beg to differ). And according to long-timers, intimacy in marriage also gets better over time if you have two people who are willing to "grow the distance" with each other.

Family Life

Tiers of Joy

Debora M. Coty

*Above all, love each other deeply, because
love covers a multitude of sins.*
1 PETER 4:8

My daughter's wedding is but a warm, fuzzy memory. Seems like it was only yesterday. Matter of fact. . .it was!

Like the shock of biting into the wooden dowels buried deep inside the towering tiers of a beautiful wedding cake, we chomped into a few jaw-breaking incidents hidden within the layers of sweet matrimonial bliss.

Our first surprise was encountering PWS syndrome: pre-wedding sweats. The bride (Christy) and MOB (moi!) underwent stress-induced personality changes during the month prior to the wedding. Normally loving and compatible, we disagreed on everything from dinnerware to formalwear.

Like shoes. What is it with shoes?

Christy abruptly halted as we headed out the door to the first bridal shower.

"Why are you wearing yucky old scuffed shoes, Mo-therrrr?" (I'm usually Mom, and they were my comfy leather sandals.) Her soft eyes turned to steel. "This is the litmus test of what you think of me. . .whether you choose to honor me by wearing your best shoes or 'dis' me with those horrible bear paws."

After ten minutes of unsuccessfully arguing the absurdity of turning my choice of footwear into a test of affection, I yielded and hobbled to the car in stiff, pinching heels. But the shoe spew wasn't through.

Next came the disagreement over four-inch spikes (which she insisted was the only solution to my cocktail-length MOB dress) or sensible pumps to accommodate three hours of dancing. She won the battle, but I won the war. The moment I limped into the reception hall, the loathsome spikes were discarded for pumps I'd concealed behind a potted palm.

Then I made the dreadful mistake of wanting to do something "different and sophisticated" with my hair for the ceremony. Amid panic attacks and sobbing jags, I went from Marilyn Monroe platinum to Morticia Adams midnight as three different stylists tried to repair what her predecessor had mangled. I ended up with a Cruella Duville motif for the most important day in my daughter's life. And we have ten thousand pictures to prove it.

Something peculiar happens to the brain during PWS. After planning the event for a full year, the normally efficient-to-the-slightest-minutia Christy forgot to order the candelabra, punch fountain, and chair bows.

When the videographer cancelled at the last minute, I substituted my cousin Ernest, who deserted his post and fled the service in the middle of the "I dos" to throw up in the bathroom. Then the sound system failed, and as the bride and groom knelt at the altar, the singers stood mutely waiting. . . and waiting. . .and waiting for their sound track to begin. It never did.

A perfect wedding is a myth. Details run amuck, tempers flare, feelings are trounced. Tiers of joy are sometimes layered with tears of frustration. But like those dowels in the wedding cake that covertly support the infrastructure, deeply embedded faith in our Omnipotent Matchmaker (God, not Aunt Myrtle) and a strong foundational relationship between a mother and daughter somehow holds everything together.

Love does cover a multitude of sins.

Except maybe shoe obsessions. . .

WORDS A WOMAN WILL NEVER SAY

"They had these coffee-beige, steel-toed boots on sale, and I just had to buy them. Their color coordinates with just about everything, and boots are so practical."

Mother Alarm

Helen Widger Middlebrooke

Giving honour unto the wife, as unto the weaker vessel.
1 PETER 3:7 KJV

The house was quiet—too quiet. In the silent darkness, a mother alarm went off—The paperboys! Had they gone back to bed? Why didn't I hear them?

I bolted out of bed and flew toward the black hallway—

BAM! A sharp pain exploded through my face and body.

"OWW!!!" I grabbed my face and fell backward. "Who shut the door?"

The scream shocked Mike awake: "What was that? What's wrong?"

"I walked into the door!"

"How did you walk into the door? Were your eyes open?"

(If they had been open years ago, this might not have happened.)

"Yes, my eyes were open. But it's dark—"

"You would have seen light down the hall."

"I'm sorry. I'm tired. I wasn't thinking," I sobbed. "I just wanted to make sure the boys were up. Why did you shut the door?"

"The boys were making too much noise."

My face felt numb and flat. I sensed blood. "Oh great. My nose is bleeding. I think I broke it."

"Do I need to take you to the emergency room?"

"It can wait for office hours. I'll put ice on it. Go back to bed."

"Right. I'll just go back to sleep while you're in pain." He paused a moment. "What do they do if it's broken? Can they put your face in a cast?"

"No, they'll put my head in a sling."

We met the paperboys by the stairs. "What happened? We heard a scream."

"Your mother ran into a door."

They wisely said nothing then, but their eyes were laughing as they followed us to the kitchen.

"You know, Mom," Matthew said, "if it didn't hurt, it would be funny."

Beneath the ice pack, the scene played out in my mind. I began to laugh. He was right—in a stupid sort of way, it was funny.

But, oh boy, did it ever hurt.

Oh Father, let me remember that the little aches and pains of life are nothing when compared with the joys of eternity, even when those I love are responsible for the hurts.

The Wood Ain't My "Hood"

Debora M. Coty

Listen to your father, who gave you life,
and do not despise your mother when she is old.
PROVERBS 23:22

I've just spent three days crammed in a tin box with my octogenarian father who gave me life and my mother "when she is old." It was not family sitcom fodder.

My RV-enthusiast parents decided that my sister Heather and I should join them for a "family" outing after a thirty-year hiatus. We arrived at our rustic campsite on the Atlantic coast—busy mothers griping that we don't have time for this—just as a cold front blew in with temperatures nipping the midthirties.

I had packed only shorts and flip-flops, anticipating the usually mild Easter week weather. Naturally, this was the year of the freak tropical Easter nor'easter. Every scrap of clothing in my suitcase became my layered uniform for the next three days. I looked like the plump filling of a s'more.

The first night I learned that the years have dealt a severe gravitational blow to the hangy-balls of my family. I had no idea three people could snore loudly enough to literally rock a camper, but they easily hit a 7 on the Richter scale. My earplugs made no dent. I spent hour after sleepless hour gritting my rattling teeth while staring at the lid of our sardine can, ineffectively elbowing my ululating sibling in the ribs on our tiny couch-bed.

Heather had somehow avoided the camping phenomena her entire pampered life, so she was quite jittery the blustery evening my father built a campfire and insisted we gather round for the Kumbaya experience. The dense woods surrounding our wee circle of firelight were teeming with wildlife, as evidenced by the rustling in the darkened bushes a few paltry feet away.

"Wh–what's out there?" wide-eyed Heather asked, brandishing a twisted wire coat-hanger-weenie-roaster like a medieval sword. "Are there. . .*bears*?"

"Nothing but armadillos, raccoons, 'possums. . .and maybe a skunk or two," I assured her in my best Grizzly Eve imitation. "Don't worry. Wild critters hate campfires."

At that moment, the pounding of paws crashing through palmetto fronds announced the arrival of a large female raccoon followed closely by a jumbo specimen with a telltale gleam in his eye. I'm assuming gender here because she apparently forgot her purse. The immutable forces of mating season drove the stampede of two directly toward, of all places, Heather's chair by the fire.

Remember that old Easter hymn, "Up from the Grave He Arose"? Well, that's the first thing that came into my head as Heather leapt screeching like a banshee atop the picnic table and commenced some sort of ancient dance ritual.

The raccoons were as amazed as the rest of us at this strange human behavior and stood upright beside Heather's overturned lawn chair, their little handlike paws hovering in midair as they gaped at the furless pink creature's performance. As my father robustly applauded and my mother burst into peals of laughter, the lady raccoon turned quizzical masked eyes to me as if to ask, "Are we supposed to throw food?"

Sometimes we get caught up in the raising of our own children and forget that we are as important to our parents as our children are to us. Our little family jaunt meant the world to my aging parents. At this stage of life, spending time together is priceless. It's never too late to make precious memories!

So despite my grousing, maybe next year I'll invest in an iPod snore blocker and neoprene body suit. And spot my sister a few tap-dancing lessons!

Boys Will Be Boys

Dena Dyer

Since we live by the Spirit, let us keep in step with the Spirit.
Let us not become conceited, provoking and envying each other.
GALATIANS 5:25–26

Do you ever find yourself burning with questions that have no answers? Such as:

How can a boy who effortlessly opens restricted e-mail files have trouble closing the toilet lid?

Why do men and boys always "flick" the remote control at the exact moment we women become interested in a program?

How can men live with dirty socks strewn all over the house but get upset if there's one empty ice tray in the freezer?

And, most importantly: Why is it that men and women are so different?

God did create us different—for a reason. It only takes a visit to a coed preschool classroom to shoot down the theory that boys and girls are alike. In one class I helped with, the boys gulped down their snacks, slapped their crafts together, and proceeded to turn blocks into guns—all within five minutes. The girls ate slowly, crafted their projects with utmost care, and then played "store" and "house."

I think life would be pretty strange, and downright sad, if both sexes were alike. Imagine if your husband were like your best girlfriend—only when he borrowed your clothes they came back all stretched out!

But how do we survive daily living with other human beings (namely, men) who sometimes seem out to get us? As one of my favorite T-shirts says, "This marriage [or family] was made in heaven—but so was thunder and lightning!"

One thing I've learned is to look for ways I'm similar to the boys in my life and build upon those. As I've pondered those things that drew my hubby and me together when we were dating (shared talents, values, and a love of enormous amounts of popcorn consumed while viewing old Andy Griffith reruns), I've tried to rekindle those "sparks" as often as possible.

And though I don't enjoy some of the things my sons do, I try to stop what I'm doing and enthusiastically partake in their passions when they ask me to. It's an honor to be asked, and I know it won't happen forever!

I also firmly believe we should affirm men in their uniqueness. Our high-speed, high-achievement culture puts enormous pressure on their shoulders, and criticism only adds to the load. A hug or a kiss can be just the ticket to letting them know we appreciate them.

I'm blessed to have a husband who shares my faith and my values. He's also wonderfully romantic and faithfully supports my own dreams and goals. My sons are affectionate, creative, smart, and hilarious. I could go on, but you get the idea. Now, if I can just say these things out loud once in a while, I'll be on the right track.

So now I have a few more questions:

When was the last time you affirmed your husband or son? If your hairstyle was completely different the last time a compliment came out of your mouth, the time is ripe to say—out loud!—the nice things you've been thinking.

How long has it been since you participated in their passions, without complaining about the sweat, dirt, or broken fingernails involved?

And, most importantly: Do you know a good place to hide the remote control?

WORDS A WOMAN WILL NEVER SAY
"I don't know, I just feel more feminine when I bait a hook with a slimy worm and fish for days in the hot sun without bathing. It's a woman thing."

Be the Glue

Michelle Medlock Adams

*A woman's family is held together by her wisdom,
but it can be destroyed by her foolishness.*
PROVERBS 14:1 CEV

Remember the old television commercial for Super Glue featuring the construction worker? The man puts glue on the top of his hard hat and glues himself to a beam. Before the commercial is through, you see that construction worker holding on to his hat, his feet dangling beneath him, several feet off the ground. Of course, the goal of this commercial is to make you think, "Wow, that glue is really strong—maybe I should buy some of that."

Super Glue is really strong stuff. I have mistakenly glued my thumb and index finger together, and, wow, was it tough to separate them! Here's my challenge to you today: Become like Super Glue for your family.

That may seem like a strange goal to you, but it's a worthy one. You should have God so big on the inside of you that His beautiful love, gorgeous goodness, and attractive acceptance emanate from you onto your family—sticking them together. In today's world, it's tough to keep a family intact. Divorce, even in the Christian community, is at an all-time high.

Children run away from home. Family members turn their backs on one another. Let's face it: The Christian family is under attack. That's why it's so important to become the glue for your family.

So how do you become the Super Glue for your family? Live out the love of Jesus in your home. Let your family see your faith. Pray for each family member every single day. Speak peace over your household. Let God bond your family together with His supreme love, and get ready to experience a beautiful home life. Pretty soon, others will ask how you "keep it all together." They'll want to know why your family is different. And you'll be able to tell them about God's love and His peace and His goodness. Your words will stick in their minds, and pretty soon they'll be the glue for their families!

Sticking it out—especially when times are tough—is rare in today's world. But as Christians, we should set the example for a beautiful, happy home life. So be the glue today!

Traveling Light

Tina Krause

"Wear my yoke—for it fits perfectly—and let me teach you;
for I am gentle and humble, and you shall find rest for your souls;
for I give you only light burdens." (Unfortunately for my husband,
I give only heavy ones.)
MATTHEW 11:29–30 TLB

"I plan to pack light on this vacation," I assured my husband as I slipped my blouses and slacks off their hangers and folded them in neat stacks inside the suitcase.

"Sure you will," he replied with a note of skepticism.

After thirty-two years of marriage and more vacations than we could afford to take, Jim knows better. My vacation checklist resembles the combined Christmas wish list of a room full of schoolchildren.

When we flew to Jamaica for a four-day stay, I filled two suitcases and a carry-on, while Jim toted one small suitcase. Men have an innate capacity for traveling light. "Just need socks, underwear, a bathing suit, and a clean shirt," he chants with the carefree demeanor of a beach bum.

But I require all the comforts of home when I hit the vacation trail. Who knows? I might need something. That's why I like to stash an ample supply of Band-Aids, aspirins, cold medicine, and a travel-size bottle of Pepto-Bismol with my snacks and sewing kit. . .just in case. While I'm fumbling through the medicine chest, gathering supplies, I fret about completing all those other tasks before leaving the house. Chores like stopping the mail and newspaper, taking the cat to Mom's, locking the windows, cleaning the house (that one puzzles Jim), and making sure the refrigerator is cleaned and emptied so that it doesn't give birth to parasitic plants while we're gone.

Truth is, it's tough for a woman to travel light. I shed unnecessary baggage about as fast as I discard cellulite. I can't help myself; preparedness is my motto. After all, who knows what shift in the weather will summon the need for sweaters and blue jeans to replace bathing suits and walking shorts? And of course shoes, which occupy an entire Pullman of their own, are my traveling staples. Reeboks for jogging (if I get around to it), sandals for casual wear, leather pumps for dress, rubber sole thongs for the beach, and at least two pair of canvas slip-ons—one white, one navy.

Jim huffed and puffed as he hauled our luggage through the airport, and he shook his head in disgust when we repeatedly had to move all the bags from one spot to another in the ticket line. Finally his frustration turned into accusatory moans. "Traveling light, huh?"

In much the same way, we ladies often have trouble traveling light spiritually, as we tote the Pullman of bitterness. Like hungry squirrels storing acorns for the winter, we store resentment to feed unforgiveness just in case we should need to defend ourselves, keep our distance, or establish our rights.

Some of us have hauled the backpack of anxiety and fear so long that worry has become second nature. Consequently, we fret about problems that are out of our control or circumstances we're unable to change.

Jesus, however, instructs us to shed the excess baggage of sin and negative emotions that weigh us down and encumber our journey. He provides rest from the heavy load long before we arrive at our final destination. The excess attitudes we tow through life are useless and destructive. That's why God instructs us to "throw off everything that hinders and the sin that so easily entangles" (Hebrews 12:1) before we allow our burdens to ruin life's trip.

With new awareness, I promised Jim that on our next trip, I would do my best to shed the excess and pack light. I've already been thinking. . .maybe if I forgo the travel iron, the bulky beach towels, and the first-aid supplies, I will (okay, Jim will) finally tote less baggage.

As for shedding the shoes. . .all right, I'll sacrifice the Reeboks.

WORDS A WOMAN WILL NEVER SAY

"I think it's about time I carried my share of the load. I'm tired of people waiting on me."

A Little Mayo with the Momwich

Anita Renfroe

"Love one another."
JOHN 13:34

There are certain things you start to say when you reach a certain age (like, "What is with all that noise on the radio?" and "Young people used to have manners in this country."). You can actually track how close you are to getting put in a nursing home by the frequency of these sorts of phrases in your daily conversations.

So, at the risk of sounding elderly, weren't the TV commercials better back in the sixties and seventies? Other than the really bad polyester outfits, the products were all designed to make our lives better and to shave the time we spent preparing meals. We had Tang—the orange flavored drink that the astronauts drank! We watched commercials for Hungry Man TV dinners, and you had your choice of mixing biscuits (Bisquick) or popping them out of a can (Pillsbury).

One of the more interesting (genderwise, that is) food commercials was one that implied a real *manly* man would never eat a regular sloppy joe *sand*wich, he needed a "Manwich" (think Tim "The Toolman" Taylor making his grunting noises). Wouldn't you think that all the bra-burning militant feminists of that era would have protested this stereotypical product labeling by boycotting Manwich? Not on your life! I have no idea what testosterone-driven ad agent thought that name would sell more sauce, but he must've been a genius because it's still on the grocery store shelves to this day.

I have experienced something slightly different than a Manwich. I have been both a bread slice and I have been the filling in what I call a "Momwich." This is a scenario where three generations of women (mother and a daughter and her daughter) all live under one roof. Sometimes it's by choice, sometimes it's of necessity, but it's always an interesting mix.

When I was two years old, my biological father left my mother and me. It was devastating for my mom, and she would have been unable to support us both had we not moved in with her parents. My mom has told me that, as my grandfather was a man given to fits of rage, she was reluctant to move back home but really had no choice financially. So it was that from the age of two until I was ten, I was the younger piece of bread in a Momwich. I have asked my mom what it was like for her to move back in with her mother at that time in her life, and she said it was a comfort to have her mom there daily during the time when she was healing from the emotional wounds of divorce and that her mother, ever the strong soul and optimist, acted as a buffer between her and her father.

My earliest childhood memories include spending lots

of time with my Nana (because my mom was working) and playing out on the farm. The days were slow, just as they should be when you are a child and have no reason to feel the passage of time. I recall feeling quite loved by my Nana and my mom (also by my grandfather, who in his older years was more docile), so this Momwich was a blessing for me and provided stability in my early life. It also gave my mom a few years of emotional haven where she could find her confidence again. My grandmother believed that God would send my mom a soul mate (since the dating pool in our little down was pret–ty small!), and Mom was resolute to hold out for someone who would love her deeply. When John Pulliam moved to Burnet to work at a fish hatchery, Mom and John fell in love and married, so the Momwich was no longer necessary. Interestingly enough, Nana would continue to spend part of the year with us when we moved from Texas to Virginia. Momwiches are enduring.

And I've found that Momwiches can morph over time, as I am now the middle part of one. I am the meaty sauce, the daughter/mother in between my mom and my daughter, and the joe can get pretty sloppy some days. When we moved to Atlanta several years ago, my parents were already in the area living on the opposite side of town. My dad's job took him on overseas trips frequently, so when Dad was out of the country Mom would stay with us so that she wouldn't have to be alone. At the same time I was starting to travel more frequently for my own work and ministry, and Mom and Dad would come over on those weekends to help out with the kids.

After a few months it occurred to us that we could save a boatload of money if we combined our incomes and bought a single house large enough for all of us. It would solve lots of problems with one fell swoop. So we found a place with three floors (so we could all ding the bell and retreat to our separate areas should the closeness start to feel—well. . .too close).

When people would hear of our arrangement they would sort of drop their jaw in amazement and ask, "How does that ever work?" And we would explain that we were all pretty busy people and hardly ever home all at the same time and we just *made* it work. My dad and my husband were great friends and all the guys would do guy things, and my mom took over the laundry room (no problem with that here!), and we just sort of agreed on what rooms got decorated by whom. Mostly no problems.

Until my mom's life changed forever.

My dad was Mom's haven, her place to vent and work things through emotionally. Tragically, about a year and a half after we moved in together, my dad died of pancreatic cancer. My mom's top part of the Momwich was scorched by grief. Within a few months of my dad's death she had surgery on her Achilles tendon and was hobbled for months. I thought it was ironic that her body mimicked her emotional state—it was like she was having to learn to walk all over again at the same time she was having to learn how to live all over again.

No longer being wife after twenty-five years of happy

marriage, Mom's core identity was suddenly undercut. I guess I shouldn't have been surprised when, in scrambling to find a sense of herself and a meaningful role in our revised family dynamic, she latched on to her intermittent Momhood with new and vigorous. . .umm. . .enthusiasm. This time around, however, she was leapfrogging a generation and aiming straight at trying to get *my* kids to toe *her* line. She had some legitimate issues about them not *always* respecting her and not *always* being as helpful as they could be, but my thoughts were, "What kids are always 100 percent in either of those areas? And what if I kinda agree with them that your standards of cleanliness might be a little high?"

Since there were some definite differences between how I was choosing to parent my kids and how I was raised, the whole issue of parenting became a huge source of contention for us for a couple of years. My mom saw some of my parenting decisions as invalidating my upbringing or not respecting the way she wanted things done, but I had definite ideas of what I thought was essential. Basically, our lists did not match, and this created a lot of tension.

My mom will be the first to admit that part of the problem was that she had raised only me. An "only." She had never dealt with multiples nor boys, so she believed everything should be as orderly and easy with three as it was with one. I, personally, enjoy chaos—at least in small doses. We no longer have as many of those issues as the boys have grown up and moved away (for most of the year). The rest of us don't make quite as big of a mess.

On the other side of my Momwich is my daughter, Elyse. She's now in her teens and can remember only a little bit of life before the Momwich. I know that her experience in this scenario is different than mine was simply because of three things: (1) She became the underlying layer later in her life (she was eight when we started the present Momwich), (2) She had older brothers in it with her, and (3) She's a different temperament than I am. Elyse is an observer and a pretty good one to get the gist of situations without much explanation. She has a high Emotional Intelligence Quotient, and she has always been her own girl.

Although she was born into a family with two older brothers, Elyse has always had a strong sense of her femininity and a firm resolve to not put up with much nonsense. She will not suffer boredom long (she regularly walks out on movies that are predictable). She knows what she likes and what doesn't fit her taste anymore. It is almost a family joke that on any given day she will just decide she doesn't like something and she will set it out into the hall, like "whenever the hall fairy comes around, she will need to pick this up and remove it from my presence." This sends her pack rat, sentimental dad into fits. He will shake his head and say, "Elyse! How could you get rid of this?" Of course, to him, everything is "special."

I know it is sometimes difficult for Elyse to be mothered by two generations at the same time. Some things are straight-up generational issues—like clothes and music tastes—and we fall out along the lines of our eras. Some differences are in our need for boundaries (Elyse needs a *lot*, I need some, Mom doesn't need any or recognize them unless you put up an electric fence). Some days I do feel the squish of the Momwich. Mom will (at times) initiate that I'm not quite getting my mom job done with Elyse in a certain area, and Elyse will be asking me to tell Mom to make herself a little more scarce when her friends come over, and *these* are the moments you wish, for a little while, that you only had one side of the bun or the other. But I love both the buns—and besides, an open face sandwich isn't on the menu right now.

But because my daughter has a strong sense of her uniqueness, I think the Momwich actually helps her to hold on to herself in a house with two other strong women. I don't think Elyse and my mom have the same sort of relations they might have if they had the normal amount of space that grandmothers and granddaughters have between them. I don't know if that is something they might miss with each other. But there is something to be said for being part of the everyday. And I wonder how it will turn out over time. We've been in our current Momwich configuration for almost a decade and we are all growing and morphing and changing and trying to remain loving through it all. Mom is moving some of her time and interests out of the house, and Elyse is perched on the edge of the nest. It's not that hard to imagine that I could be the top bun in another kind of Momwich someday.

I also wonder how many women find themselves, at different times in their lives, in a Momwich. It certainly isn't something you dream about as a child. I don't think anyone, when she is seven years old and dreaming about her adult life says, "Man, I can't wait to grow up so I can keep living with my mother!" But life brings to us situations that change our idea of "normal" and give us a chance to see whether the faith and grace we profess to possess is all talky, talky and no walky, walky. And it gives a daily proving ground for love to triumph through dysfunction.

I've found that Momwiches are a lot like Manwiches: meaty, messy, alternately sloppy, and satisfying. Like the Manwich, a Momwich is a slightly heavier emotional portion that many would not even attempt to bite off, but we are all three the stronger women for it.

Motherhood

Inheriting the Family Jewels

Debora M. Coty

Tell to the generation to come the praises of the LORD,
and His strength and His wondrous works that He has done.
PSALM 78:4 NASB

There are many kinds of heirlooms: priceless china, ruby pendants, even Great-Grandma's corset (they sure don't make 'em like that anymore—hallelujah!).

Not all that we inherit from our foremothers is a source of familial pride. My knobby knees, varicose veins, and feisty disposition, for example, are straight from Granny Nell. Three generations have done nothing to drain the gene pool.

Despite vehement protests to the contrary, I see signs of my twenty-one-year-old daughter, Christy, turning into me. Same expressions, body language, even eating habits.

After ridiculing me for years about indulging in Cheetos as my before-dinner hors d'oeuvre (you can eat most anything if you call it a hors d'oeuvre), I recently caught Christy sneaking a few crunchy specimens of her own.

"It's not a habit, Mom, I can quit any time I want."

Yeah, right. That's what all the addicts say.

Just yesterday, the little darlin' was mortified when I

smugly pointed out that her hands were resting palm-up in her lap like dead roaches. This was the same term she'd always used while rolling her eyes and strongly advising me to "turn your hands over, Mom, and *try* to be normal."

And then there's her newfound insistence on lists. For years, Sugar Dumpling made fun of my lists and sticky notes everywhere. There are four to six stuck to my purse flap at any given moment. "Mom, you have notes to see other notes—your purse looks like a piñata!"

When she invited me over to her new apartment last week, I counted—discreetly, of course—three sticky notes on her counter and two more on her purse. Ha! The apple falling from the tree may have attempted to chuck itself across the orchard, but it rolled right back to the trunk.

Although I am secretly honored that my daughter is following in my footsteps, there's a sobering sense of responsibility, too. As a Christian mother, I believe that faith is the most important legacy to pass down to my children—a vibrant, living faith, far more priceless than any jewel.

But it's all too easy to let circumstances and hardships tarnish that inestimable gem. My children have front row seats to my life; they will *know* if my faith plays out as genuine or counterfeit.

As fallible mothers, we can only pray that our lapses in judgment, failures, and mistakes witnessed by our children are overshadowed by their observance of God's grace, mercy, and forgiveness in our lives. Only through His power can we pass on the legacy of faith to future generations.

We can't always control our children's heritage. If our kids inherit our worst attributes, they can hide their knobby knees beneath pants, strip their varicose veins, and take anger management classes. But the essence of Jesus in their lives—now *that's* a keepsake!

Smotherly Love

Anita Renfroe

Above all, love each other deeply.
1 PETER 4:8

When you are a baby it's comforting
 When you are a kid it seems annoying.
When you are a teenager you think you will die of it.
When you are an adult it seems insulting.

It is the difficulty mothers have judging distance between themselves and their child. If they are going to err it's almost always on the side of too close. This is a problem that's almost tied into emotions and geography. Kids start off as close as they can possibly be—inside of us. All it takes for either mom or daughter to acknowledge this intimate connection is a glance at the little wrinkly divot in the middle of our middles (or, for some of you "outies" a little bump in the belly landscape). Belly buttons remind us that we came from somewhere, some*one*, and that we were not hatched, we were attached. Our physical detachment is marked by this funny little belly button, but we all have to gradually detach emotionally from the Maternal Unit.

You can talk about being Daddy's Girl all you want, but whether the chips are down or the gloves are off, moms and daughters are attached. Sometimes it's like two polecats with their tails tied tossed over a clothesline, but we are attached. We are the girls of the house, bound by gender, cosmetics, hair issues, and hormones.

Once our daughters move outside of us we have a little separation, but we still keep them very near to us night and day. Then they start crawling and they starting moving away from us, and we still keep them in our sights. Then they start walking and it starts with the walking toward us so that they can fall into our arms, but it eventually leads to walking away from us. We are taught by experience that things happen when they are away from us that cause them to run back to us requiring first aid. This makes us nervous. Then a school bus takes them away for part of the day. Then the driver's license allows them to go farther. Then it's time to move away, and a mom's heart has never really gotten past the fact that you crawled away all those years ago.

Let's get real—moms would like to hang on to their job. It has been one defining aspect of our life for a good while. If you have been looking out for your well-being for double digits you have to admit that instinct might be a little difficult to turn off without some fits and starts and sputters. We don't really want our children tied to our apron strings, but if they could just hang on by a leeetle thread that wouldn't be so terrible, would it?

All of this makes for some difficult navigations through the "series of gradually harder good-byes." It's not that moms set out to smother you, it's just that they don't really know how to stop. It is hard to develop healthy emotional distance from someone when you were her Womb Raider for the first months of your existence. And when you surfaced, this woman was your caretaker and guardian. She lived in her own versions of the movie *Groundhog Day* during your toddler years and answered your kajillion questions as you came into early childhood. Your mom served as your moral compass, Jiminy Cricket, and Impossible Rule Maker when you were a teen and helped you chart out a plan to create independence as a young adult. So why is it so hard to understand why she has a difficult time letting go? It is safe to say that the woman who changed your millionth diaper and rode with you when you had your learner's permit is probably going to have a hard time seeing you as fully adult.

But daughters feel a powerful drive to separate to autonomy and can't wait to fire their emotional rocket boosters and achieve their own adult orbit. For some this happens earlier in their teens and causes a good bit of drama as the timetables for finishing school and financial independence don't always sync up with their feelings of restlessness.

I remember being so conflicted as a teenage daughter. I knew that I wasn't quite grown yet, but I wanted to be so badly. It's like you are spending all your time on the launching pad and you are just itching for the NASA countdown. I see it in my own daughter. She sometimes feels restless and unsettled. She loves being the princess here at home but knows that season is winding down for her. It is bittersweet and a time of inner conflict for mothers and daughters, this letting out of the emotional lifeline.

And daughters may feel anxious about revealing their personal changes to us and wonder how we will respond. My friend Ellie relates a funny story about such an instance with her daughter:

Paris came home on Thanksgiving weekend for her freshman year break. She shared late Thursday night that she really needed to talk to me and that it was important. The weekend got busy with food and friends and visits, and she insisted Sunday morning that we absolutely needed to talk. I saw the intensity in her eyes and took her inside a locked room. I grabbed both hands and locked eyes and urged her to share and apologized for making her wait three days.

Her eyes finally settled on mine after looking away a few times.

"What is it, baby? What's troubling you?"

"Mom. . .Mom. . .I'm. . .I'm. . .Mom, I'm not a Republican anymore!"

I held her close and breathed a deep sigh.

"Don't you worry—we'll love you no matter what, and we'll work it out."

And, as daughters, we can become living embodiments of the Elvis song, "Suspicious Minds." We think that our mom wants to know everything about us just so she can continue to direct our lives with this knowledge (for some this may be true, but it's probably the exception). Mothers are the people who find every minute detail of their daughter's life interesting. Daughters are the people who find this trait almost impossible to appreciate.

This has been a difficult issue for my mom and me because of my mom's particular gifts. She loves to make home an inviting, warm, hospitable place to be and has been an integral part of our ability to have a ministry that is sometimes away from home for the last several years. That meant that, because she lives with us, her knowledge of our life was far more extensive than if she lived in another town or another state. I remember the day I totally went off on my mom because this came to a head. I was feeling resentful because of all the things she was privy to. She has supersensitive hearing for water running, so she literally knows every time someone turns on a faucet or if the toilet handle sticks in our house. And every phone call that comes in. And every piece of mail that comes in and every person that comes to the door and every time I go to the mall and every time I have a cold. It's not that she *shouldn't* know that stuff, it's just not *normal* for her to know it without my telling her. That's really just too much knowledge for anyone other than your spouse. And normally even *he* doesn't know all that. As thankful as I was for my mom's presence in our home so that we could travel and minister part of the time, it was time to ask for some voluntary boundaries.

This is difficult for mothers and daughters. When I

would feel it was time to discuss this with my mom I would literally put it off for weeks because I knew she would view it as ungrateful on my part. When daughters ask for space it's hard for a mom to believe that it's not driven by disloyalty or selfishness. But I can say from my own experience that it is essential to feel that your life is your own. As much as you love your mother and want to have an intimate lifelong relationship with her, there are portions of your life that must be separate to be healthy. The amount of emotional space it takes to have a feeling of adult-ness and autonomy will vary from relationship to relationship. But from time to time, new boundaries will have to be set up and honored.

In my situation, because my mom lives here, we have found that it's necessary to decide what is important to each female and figure out our preferences and nonnegotiables. It is important to identify them and to talk with your mother about them. For my mom, she loves, loves, LOVES to do laundry. She will go around the house and solicit different kinds of clothes for loads she is "getting up" (this is a concept that makes perfect sense to her, but I cannot understand why anyone would want to "get up" a load). This turns into a game of Laundry Go Fish.

"Anybody got any darks?"

"No, Mom. I've got a delicate and a towel but no darks. Go fish."

She does loads of laundry pretty much every day and enjoys it immensely. I would only do laundry if no one in our house had clean underwear *and* Target was closed so that we couldn't buy any. Just how stupid it would be of me to insist that she let me do laundry two days a week just so I could make a point about having some ownership of the laundry room. I know that's not important to me. I know that it's important to her. She can have it.

By the same token, my mom agonizes over making large purchases. She will look and look and look for curtains or furniture, she will decide and then second-guess her decisions. She will bring stuff home and take it back several times before she decides that she doesn't like any of it. Not me. I can sweep through a store and make decisions in a single day and feel confident that I got the right thing and enjoy it. This doesn't stress me in the least. How foolish it would be of her to insist that she go with me to make large purchases for our home? A willingness to give and take and the self-knowledge to discern what is important goes a long way toward peaceful coexistence.

I realize that most of the mothers and daughters reading this do not have our living arrangements, but the principles are the same. When your mom comes to visit you can have the same sort of feeling of encroachment if you haven't figured our what is truly important to you and what areas you could just allow your mom to be free in. Everything is not important. Not every hill is worth dying on. Some areas aren't your forte and it doesn't really matter to you one way or the other. Is there some place we could meet and live in harmony here?

One problem we have between mothers and daughters is that we haven't fully thought about what we need. I think we need gullies. Gullies are usually created by rain.

My mom and my daughter both love rain. They love it for different reasons, but their response to rain is much the same. My mom is a farmer's daughter and will actually clap her hands like a child on Christmas morning when she hears the rain start to fall on our skylights in the kitchen. She will watch the Weather Channel just so she can see the patterns of clouds passing over us, around us, south, or north of us. When we call in from another state to check in she will tell us, "There was a little cloud right over us, and it looked like we were going to get a little something, but it passed us by and we got nothing. Not even a drop."

My daughter loves rain because she thinks dark days are the best. She is an indoors chick and the rain means she will be inside all day. Plus she likes to nap and cloudy days are just conducive to great napping. In this way I am sure that I had some genetic influence in her life, even though I am an all-weather napper.

But rain is what makes gullies—actually it's the runoff from the rain. It's not as large as a stream or a river, just an oversized ditch that separates two pieces of land and allows the excess rain to run off and not damage the structures on either side. When I think of what I want with my mom and what I believe my daughter will want as an adult with me, I think of a gully. It's nicely formed with enough distance for distinct separation but not so much that you can't jump across should a situation warrant it. It's also a place where excess emotion can run off from conversations and situations without damaging each of us permanently.

There are times when we react to situations and use an emotional nuclear device to create something that is an unmeasured response. We drop a "bomb" to display our need for space and end up with a divide that is too wide to get across and stand on the other side wondering what happened—we now have a Grand Canyon instead of a gully. Then there comes a time when we desperately need the affection and comfort that only our mom can give us, but we have left no way to cross over. The span is just too wide.

I think it falls to the grown daughter to consider the distance of the division you need between yourself and your mom. Given the way the relationship starts out, it is easy to see how the idea of separation is so much more difficult for the mom than for the daughter. Daughters' lives are about carving out more autonomy and freedom. As a rule, mothers' lives are spent grieving and adjusting to whatever new level their girl is creating. As much as your mom wants you to live your new life, she would still like to be included more than you would probably feel comfortable allowing. It is hard to make gullies instead of canyons when you are reacting to the feeling that your life needs wider emotional margins of separation.

If a mother and daughter have a strong relationship and both try to follow biblical principles the theory is that this whole negotiation should be easier, but I'm not sure it is. We need shovelfuls of self-respect and courage to get the gullies started, walls of love and mutual respect to keep them from becoming too large, the emotional rains to wash them out and keep them clean and free flowing, and the connection that comes from inviting each other to jump the gully every now and then.

If only we could make a temporary perspective shift where we could somehow get into each other's brain for a few minutes, we would be able to see that the smotherly love is not meant to infringe and the daughterly need for boundaries isn't meant to shut out. The ties that bind us are enduring, endearing, and just a little bit maddening. *C'est la vie femme. Viva la différence!*

Beauty

Throwing in the Jowl

Debora M. Coty

Charm is deceptive, and beauty is fleeting;
but a woman who fears the LORD is to be praised.
PROVERBS 31:30

At age forty-nine, I decided to reinvent myself. Revise. Overhaul. Make over. I figured life is one long revision anyway.

As a teen in the seventies, my best friend Tiffany had the ethereal beauty and grace of Olivia Newton John. I, on the other hand, had the ethereal beauty and grace of Elton John. So I discovered makeup, high heels, and the friendly Whack-A-Do hair stylist.

Then life happened and chic-factor dropped to the bottom of my priority list behind marriage, kids, and career. Several decades later, I was still using Cover Girl makeup and sporting the same clothing styles and long scraggly hairdo held back with alligator clips that I wore in my senior class picture.

At my twenty-fifth high school reunion, I won the "Least Changed" prize. This was not a good thing.

There's nothing sadder than a middle-aged woman looking like a teen wannabe.

The need to update slammed me head-on when my sixteen-year-old daughter and I were looking through old photographs taken before her birth and counted eight blouses that I still owned. In fact, I was wearing one at that very moment! Despite protests that I was just trying to get my money's worth, she dragged me to the mall and supervised the purchase of five "hot" shirts (with these hot flashes, I'm already a hot mama), two pairs of jeans (that weren't painter's pants), and a purse that didn't resemble a diaper bag on steroids.

The hair was another can of worms. Literally. I've yet to comprehend why God allows hormones to do such a nasty number on once-shiny hair as we age, when all our other body parts are either plunging south or expanding like minute rice in a pot of soup.

The writer of Proverbs wasn't kidding about fleeting beauty!

During my self-neglect years, I simply hacked my own ponytail when it reached an unmanageable length. By the time I sought professional help, there was not much to work with. My stylist tried perming my frizz once called hair. Think Chia Pet. Taming treatments resulted in a serpentine Medusa look. Layers created a strange resemblance to the Christmas trees I drew in third grade. I spent so much time in my stylist's chair, she named a blow dryer after me.

I was sorely tempted to shear my head and drop off wigs for servicing.

Tiffany and I made a pact that the year we turned fifty,

we'd get face-lifts together. But she's backing out. Why not? The bags under her eyes aren't even totes, much less trunks like mine. She still looks like Olivia in her *Grease* days. Unblemished skin, gentle laugh creases instead of inch-deep furrows, one chin. . .

I inherited my grandfather's jowls, which jiggle like a turkey's wattle when I move. Holding my head queenly high in pictures reduces my triple chin to one, but when I bow my head to read or pray, it looks like a wad of bread dough has sprouted from my neck.

So instead of a face-lift, I'm considering alligator clips behind my ears.

God assures us that all this doesn't matter. Despite conflicting cultural messages, our relationship with Him is all that *really* counts. And His rejuvenating touch of joy creates the ultimate face-lift!

Laughter and Hairpins

Michelle Medlock Adams

*He will yet fill your mouth with laughter
and your lips with shouts of joy.*
JOB 8:21

Like most women, I like to look my best when I leave the house. So when I received the worst haircut of my life a few years ago, I was panicked! I had a mullet. To improve my hairstyle during the growing out process, I bought some faux hair that matched my natural hair. It sort of clipped in my natural hair, but it took me awhile to get the hang of it.

Imagine this. . .I'm in the office of a coworker, discussing the outcome of a meeting we'd just had in the conference room, and as I went over a point very passionately, I flipped my hair. In fact, I flipped it right off my head. My faux hair landed on the ground, near my coworker's feet. She jumped and screamed a bit. (I think she thought it was a gopher or something.) We both laughed until our stomachs hurt.

I learned a valuable lesson that day—well, two actually. First off, it's good to laugh at yourself. And second, always use a lot of bobby pins when securing faux hair.

Laughing together and showing your vulnerability can be very bonding. Don't be afraid to be imperfect with your coworkers and God. They'll love you—mullet and all.

God Loves Airheads, Too

Debora M. Coty

Who in the world do you think you are to second-guess God? Do you for one moment suppose any of us knows enough to call God into question? Clay doesn't talk back to the fingers that mold it, saying, "Why did you shape me like this?"
ROMANS 9:20 MSG

Before I spoke at a women's brunch, an icebreaker was passed out. You were supposed to check off which of the eighteen behaviors you'd ever performed, including such classics as "locked yourself out of the house," "gone somewhere wearing two different shoes," "put something unusual in the refrigerator," "lost someone while shopping," "dialed a phone number and forgot who you called," and "called a family member by the wrong name."

I was mortified to discover that I'd done every single thing on the page—*within the last month!*

My daughter, who was accompanying me, lost no time in reminding me of the well-chilled iron she'd found in the refrigerator the day before and the electronic keypad we'd installed because I kept stranding myself in the yard.

"And remember when you called Grandma last Tuesday and asked who she was and why you wanted to talk to her?"

"Hush, Rocky—er, I mean Christy," I whispered, glancing at my feet to make sure I'd changed the bedroom slippers my husband had pointed out as I was leaving the house. While the good ladies were tallying votes, it seemed like a dandy time to escape to the bathroom.

Discombobulated (and who wouldn't be after realizing you were the Airhead Queen?), I forgot that I'd clipped my microphone amplifier to my high-top grannies and gave myself a major wedgie when I attempted to use the facilities. At first tug, the amp box shot into the air above the john. Diving to rescue it from a watery grave, my glasses slid into the bosom of my dress. As I rooted around my cleavage, I felt my bra clasp pop. Heavy sigh.

Unfortunately, this little scenario is nothing new. Life is so. . .daily.

I've often wondered why God made me this way, only to become frustrated and envious as I compare myself to other women who seem to have it all together. Am I defective? Did God forget to hook me up to the voltmeter when He wired my brain? Why does everyone else remember names and faces and I'm reduced to introducing decade-long friends as, "Leanne and Michael, and their children. . .(embarrassing silence). . .their children."

I frantically play back tapes of my memory, but all I see is gray fuzz.

And it's not only my memory, it's decision making, too. As I catapult toward that half-century mark in age, I'm finding it harder and harder to choose wisely. I used to pride myself on quick, logical judgments: the green shoes or the teal? The teal, of course—they'll match more of my clothes. Now I just stare slack-jawed at the shoe store and go home with every color in the catechism. My husband thinks I'm indecisive, but I'm just not sure.

While recently admiring the simplistic beauty of my favorite terra-cotta vase, I realized although it wasn't Ming or Tiffany, it was lovely in its own right—not worse, not inferior. . .just different. I couldn't imagine that humble vessel lambasting the potter who made it practical instead of pricey, useful instead of ornamental. That vase gracefully fulfilled its purpose, and I would choose it in a heartbeat over any collectable.

The Master Potter reminded me that I, cracked pot that I am, am not worse or inferior than others, but lovely in my own right. Special and useful to Him. Maybe even His favorite vase *because* of my flaws.

After all, He made me just as I am.

Makeup—Don't Leave Home without It

Michelle Medlock Adams

"The Lord does not look at the things man looks at. Man looks at the outward appearance, but the Lord looks at the heart."
1 Samuel 16:7

My pastor leaned over the pulpit, smiled, and said, "I always tell my wife to treat her makeup like the commercial says to treat your American Express card—don't leave home without it!"

I glanced over at his wife and thought, *Yep. He is so sleeping on the pastoral couch tonight.*

All teasing aside, the dog may be man's best friend, but mascara is a lady's best bud. My mama always told me to put on a little lipstick and some mascara at the very least, because you never know who you might run into at the grocery store. She's right, of course. The one time I headed to Wal-Mart without a speck of makeup on, I practically saw my entire high school graduating class. I wanted to hide in the display of toilet paper until all the lights were dimmed and I could bolt to my car. Ever been there?

Makeup is an amazing thing. It can hide blemishes. It can enhance your eyes. It can make thin lips look luscious and moist. It can transform stubby, faded eyelashes into long, curled, and dark lashes. It can give your cheeks color, making you appear well rested when you've been up all night. Makeup is a gift from God—I'm sure of it!

But wouldn't it be even better if our skin had no flaws to cover? Wouldn't it be better if our lips were already the perfect shade of pink? Wouldn't it be better if our cheeks were naturally rosy and our lashes naturally thick? If we were already perfect, we wouldn't need anything to cover our imperfections.

Well, maybe our outsides aren't perfect, but if you've asked Jesus to be your Lord and Savior, your heart is blemish-free. See, God didn't just cover our sins with His heavenly Father foundation. Instead, He sent Jesus to die for us and take away all of our sins. Isn't that good news? The moment we asked Jesus to forgive us, we became blemish-free on the inside.

That's how God sees us—perfect and blemish-free. The Word says that God looks on the heart, while man looks on the outward appearance. So while you might want to put a little paint on the barn before venturing out, your heart is already lovely.

Words a Woman Will Never Say

"I prefer to reveal my age spots and facial flaws so that my true inner beauty is free to shine through."

Bring On the Legwarmers

Michelle Medlock Adams

Jesus Christ is the same yesterday and today and forever.
HEBREWS 13:8

Ahhh. . .the eighties. I remember them well. I graduated from Bedford, Indiana's North Lawrence High School in 1987, so I am an eighties lady. Oh yeah. I had hair so big I could hardly fit into my red Fiero. I practically had to use a can of hair spray a day to keep those big ol' bangs sky-high. I wore the neon-colored plastic bracelets up my arms—just like Madonna. And I even had a pair of leg warmers. Scary, huh? Yeah, my daughters think my senior yearbook is pretty hilarious.

Even if you're not an eighties lady, I bet there were some fashion fiascos from your time, too. For example, what was with that caked-on baby blue eye shadow of the seventies? Yuck!

Fashion trends come and go. One week, the fashion magazines say, "Long jackets are hip. The longer the better. . ." and the next week, the fashion trend reads, "Cropped, military-style jackets are the rage! Long coats are short on fashion savvy. . ." Ugh! Let's face it. It's almost impossible to keep up with the times.

Fads come and go. Styles change. And the way clothes fit our bodies definitely changes over time. (Can I hear an "Amen"?) Change is inevitable. From changing fashions to changing locations to changing diapers—as women, we're in the "changing" mode most of our lives. So in the midst of all this change, isn't it good to know that God never changes? Malachi 3:6 says, "I the LORD do not change."

You can always count on the Lord. He's there through thick and thin, leg warmers and parachute pants, and everything in between. Let Him be the stability in your life. Run to God when you feel overwhelmed by the changes going on around you. If you'll stay grounded in Him, you'll always be "heavenly hip" and ready to face anything—even if spandex stirrup pants make a comeback!

Blind Faith

Michelle Medlock Adams

I am sure that nothing can separate us from God's love—
not life or death, not angels or spirits, not the present or the future.
ROMANS 8:38 CEV

Let's be honest. There are some beauty tricks that simply don't make sense if you think about them too long. In fact, some of them are downright gross. For instance, if you have tired, puffy eyes from too many sleepless nights, you're supposed to pat a little Preparation H under your eyes to reduce the puffiness and rejuvenate your tired peepers.

Yes, it's quite effective, but did you ever think you'd use hemorrhoid cream around your eyes? Me either! Or how about the old Vaseline-on-the-teeth trick? Beauty queens have known about this tip for years! You simply put a little slimy Vaseline over your front teeth to create a shinier smile onstage. Of course, it feels yucky, but it works!

Sometimes you just have to have blind faith and try these odd beauty tricks. There's no rhyme or reason to them, and they may even seem gross to you. But if you try them, you'll discover they actually work.

You know, some of the teachings in the Bible seem odd, too. Take Matthew 5:38–44, for example. Instead of an "eye for eye, and tooth for tooth," we are supposed to love our enemies: "You have heard that it was said, 'Eye for eye, and tooth for tooth.' But I tell you, Do not resist an evil person. If someone strikes you on the right cheek, turn to him the other also. And if someone wants to sue you and take your tunic, let him have your cloak as well. If someone forces you to go one mile, go with him two miles. . . . Love your enemies and pray for those who persecute you."

Hmm. Not exactly what human nature tells us to do, right? Sometimes you just have to trust and go forward in blind faith. If you're a very practical person, this might be hard for you, so ask God to help you follow His ways even when they seem outlandish or uncomfortable. He will! He is the Father of faith, and He has more than enough to fill you up so that you can step out in blind faith and love your enemies, pray for those who despitefully use you, and go that extra mile.

So take a risk. Go against your human nature and step out in blind faith both in the natural and the spiritual. You'll have rested eyes, shiny teeth, and a beautiful spirit!

No-Makeup Day

Tina Krause

Faith without works is dead.
(And a day without makeup is anything but glorious!)
JAMES 2:20 KJV

"Oh, it was glorious," my friend beamed as she told me about her no-makeup day. I was envious. The thought of awaking in the morning to snub my cosmetic case was more enticing to me than feasting on a box of chocolates in the midst of a sugar attack.

But before I could schedule "my day," I had to mentally prepare myself. *Men don't worry about cosmetics, so why should women?* I reasoned. *Besides, why gob mascara on perfectly clean eyelashes and draw dark lines on my eyelids like a road map? Yeah, that's right! I'm tired of painting my face to please others! Au natural is the real me!*

All pumped up, my day arrived. Eager to nix my feminine fixation, I tossed my powder puff and blush brush to the wind. Gleefully, I splashed water on my face, patted it dry, swept my hair into a tousled ponytail, and voila! Freedom. Barefaced and beautiful (all in the eye of the beholder, remember?), I faced my face with confidence.

But soon my protest posed a slight problem. It began with

the doorbell. On my day of nonconformity a pushy salesman and two unexpected visitors flocked to my door to test my resolve. Feeling less confident, I scurried to the grocery store for a gallon of milk, hoping I wouldn't see anyone I knew. Not a chance. There she was in all her flawless beauty and fashion flare, an acquaintance I hadn't seen in years. As I lurked behind a store display, she flagged me down, gushing with waves and chatter.

"Well hello! How are you?" she surged with her cover-girl smile, as I struggled to adjust my lopsided ponytail. In true freedom, I apologized for my appearance, assuring her I never look that way. But I doubt she heard me.

Driving home, I began to question my glorious makeup-less state, but I gave myself a short pep talk. With new resolve, I attacked the rest of my day with renewed assurance. After all, I was safely home now.

Peering out the front window, I noticed the mail truck pull away, so I walked outside to the mailbox. Right on cue, my neighbor pulled out of his driveway to leave his house. I knew I could get by with a brief wave, but just in case, I bowed my head to sort through my stack of mail as if I hadn't noticed him. No go. This was the one time he stopped to talk, which meant I had to approach his car, giving him an up-close-and-personal view of my barefaced state. Not only that, I had just eaten a kosher dill with lunch, which meant my breath reeked of pickle juice. Preoccupied with my sloppy appearance and pungent pickle breath, I had no idea what he said.

No more pep talks. The moment I stepped indoors, I

dashed to the bathroom to brush my teeth, style my hair, and apply the Maybelline, even though I knew I wouldn't see another soul all day. It mattered little. The act of primping compensated for how humiliated I felt after allowing the masses to see me pale-faced and frumpy.

Funny thing about nonconformity; unless you believe in your cause, the act is more ineffective than the roar of a toothless lion. Similar to our walk with the Lord. We believe in Jesus Christ, yet do we demonstrate our faith through corresponding deeds? When we defy conformity to the world, we should be unashamed to speak the truth even when challenged, faced with opposition, or when things occur to test our resolve. Our convictions come from the heart, based on the truth of God's Word, so negativity fails to intimidate us. Unlike my makeupless state, our spiritual transparency doesn't humiliate us; rather, we freely communicate the gospel despite our flaws.

Good point to remember the next time I risk another no-makeup day. Insecurity, humiliation, and lack of conviction quell the whole meaning behind cosmetic abstinence. Add to that the scent of pickle juice, and nonconformity takes on a whole, ah, new complexion. . . .

God Loves You—Flaws and All

Michelle Medlock Adams

*So let's come near God with pure hearts and
a confidence that comes from having faith.*
HEBREWS 10:22 CEV

If you listen closely, you can hear them. Women around the globe, groaning and moaning in dressing rooms. Are they in pain? Are they ill? No, it's just bathing suit season, and they're trying to find the one perfect suit that doesn't make them look fat. It's a quest every woman embarks on, and it's one of the most daunting tasks she will ever face.

Seriously, is there anything more humbling than standing in front of a dressing room mirror, under those unforgiving fluorescent lights, trying on bathing suit after bathing suit? I think not. I dread it every year. Because no matter how many miles you've logged in previous months, no matter how many crunches you've crunched, no matter how many desserts you've passed up, bathing suits show every imperfection. While you might be able to hide a few dimples underneath blue jeans or a nice black dress, you're not hiding anything in a bathing suit.

That's pretty much how it is with God. You might be able to fake grin your way through church. You might be able to "play Christian" in front of your friends and family. But when you enter the throne room, it's like wearing your bathing suit before God. You can't hide any imperfections from Him. He sees it all. That truth used to horrify me—even more than trying on bathing suits—but not anymore.

Here's the great thing about God. He gave us Jesus to take care of our sin, because God knew we'd be flawed. No matter how many good deeds we do, no matter how many chapters of the Bible we read each day, and no matter how many casseroles we bake for church functions, we can never be good enough for God. We can't earn our way into God's favor. All we have to do is ask Jesus to be the Lord of our lives, and we're "in." Then, whenever we enter the throne room, God sees us through "the Jesus filter," and all He sees is perfection. If you haven't asked Jesus to take away your sin and be the Lord of your life, why not take care of that today? It's the most wonderful step you'll ever make.

Now, if we could just figure out some kind of perfection filter for bathing suit season, life would be super.

Step into the Light

Michelle Medlock Adams

"This is the crisis we're in: God-light streamed into the world, but men and women everywhere ran for the darkness. They went for the darkness because they were not really interested in pleasing God."
JOHN 3:19 MSG

Have you ever been in a situation where you've had to do your makeup in a dim room? Sometimes when I travel, the lighting in the hotel room isn't so great. I put on my makeup as best I can, but when I get into the car and look at myself in the bright sunlight, I am horrified. Many times, I have on way too much blush or eye makeup, but because of the dark hotel room, I had no idea I looked like Bozo in drag. I thought I was looking pretty good, but the natural light told me differently. Light is a powerful thing. It reveals much about us. This is also true in spiritual matters.

The Bible says that Jesus is the Light of the World. When we look to Him and His Word, it also reveals much about us. Through His Word you may find areas of darkness in your life that you weren't even aware existed. The Lord may shine His light on bitterness that's been hiding in a dark corner of your heart. Or the Lord may shine His light on that unforgiveness you've been harboring for years. If you've been living in darkness for some time, looking into the Light of the Word of God can be quite scary! You'll see many flaws in yourself. (You may find that you also look like Bozo in drag, spiritually speaking.)

But don't run from Jesus and the Bible when you see your flaws and shortcomings. Instead, embrace the truth and ask Him to get rid of the flaws that He exposed. God wants you to live free from that mess. That's why He has illuminated the situation for you. Finding out you have areas that need work is the first step to recovery, right?

Let Jesus and His light fill you up and flow out of you. Continue to look into the Word and allow His light to reveal areas where you need growth. As you do this, you'll find that you are being transformed from Bozo to Beauty. Talk about an extreme makeover! Bring it on!

Pale Legs Springtime Struggle

Tina Krause

Can any hide himself in secret places that I [God] shall not see him?
(No, Lord, not even beneath baggy sweats and
oversized shirts; but would You mind not shining
so brightly upon my pale, lard-laden legs?)
JEREMIAH 23:24 KJV

Each spring, more than daylilies and daffodils burst from winter's darkness. Pale legs, shaded from the summer sun, also appear at the first balmy rise in temperature. Some pop out, others plop, but they surface just the same.

For the ploppers among us, this is spring's first struggle— a time when we refuse to wear shorts as a matter of dignity. Colorless legs are bad enough, but ones that resemble dimpled elephant stumps are enough to cause some of us to pray for an arctic blast in mid-June.

So in late spring I join those who laboriously catch the rays to tan their shapeless lard-laden legs. A bronze tone compensates for the lack of firm, been-sweating-in-the-gym-all-winter thighs, I reason. But experience reminds me that bumpy cellulite comes in all colors. You can tan it, tone it, slip nylons over it to hold it together, but short of liposuction, it's a lost cause.

I am preoccupied with camouflaging human flaws, nonetheless. I apply makeup and creams to contour my face, conceal wrinkles, and firm droopy eyelids tauter than a soldier's army bunk. Oversized shirts hide my midsection, and baggy jeans lose heavy hips in a sea of denim.

Eventually, however, the camouflage is removed. The Maybelline is washed off at the end of the day, and unshed pounds make their seasonal debut in the summer's sun. As the adage goes, "You can run, but you can't hide." At least not for long.

But I try anyway, even with more "weighty" matters than physical flaws. I often try to conceal poor attitudes and bad habits with spiritual clichés and Sunday smiles, but sooner or later the summer sunshine of God's Holy Word exposes my spiritual lumps and jiggles.

Spring's first struggle is often undignified. . .but it's necessary. We may deny it, cover it, or boast our Sunday best and act like it isn't there, but sooner or later our spiritual imperfections surface.

However, there is hope: When our flaws meet the Son, Christ promises to forgive, heal, firm, and reshape our lives so that we'll never have to hide again.

So whisk out the shorts and struggle no more. It's springtime!

Expert Opinions—No Thanks!

Michelle Medlock Adams

Then I heard a loud voice saying in heaven, "Now salvation, and strength, and the kingdom of our God, and the power of His Christ have come, for the accuser of our brethren, who accused them before our God day and night, has been cast down."
REVELATION 12:10 NKJV

Actress Debra Messing, who is known for her beauty, shared that she was always a little self-conscious about her looks, but after she became famous and sat in a makeup artist's chair every day, she said she learned she had more flaws than she'd ever realized. "The experts" were quick to point out her flaws and what they'd have to do to make her appear flawless. Talk about scary!

It's kind of like *Ambush Makeover* on Fox. Have you ever seen that show? You leave the house thinking you look pretty good, then suddenly you're ambushed by "an expert" who begins telling you that your hair is frizzy, your makeup is all wrong, and you look stupid in your ripped jeans. Ugh! *Please* don't sign me up for that show. (I think I'll go with the ignorance is bliss approach on this one!)

There's one thing for sure: The world is full of "experts" who will happily point out your flaws—even if you don't ask for their expert opinions. Sometimes those experts are in your family. You go to the annual family picnic and your aunt Lucy says, "Ooh, you've put on a lot of weight since last year. I read where you should drink more water to lose weight fast—can I get you a bottle of water, dear?" Or your best friend says, "I recently read about a new wrinkle cream that is guaranteed to diminish crow's-feet. I cut out the ad for you." Nice, huh? Oh yes, we love those expert opinions.

Yep, experts lurk around every corner. The devil even fancies himself as an expert. He loves to point out all of your flaws. The Bible says that he is an accuser of the brethren. In other words, he loves to tell you what a crud ball you are because if he can convince you that you're a crud ball, he knows you'll never live out the beautiful life that God has planned for you. Like most of these so-called experts, the devil's opinion is worth about as much as the gum on the bottom of your shoe. Ignore him! You may not be perfect, but you're perfectly saved. You're perfectly loved by God. And if you've asked Jesus to be your Lord and Savior, your heart is flawless. So take that, devil! We're hot! And you just live where it's hot.

Reality

Toni Sortor

The glory of young men is their strength,
gray hair the splendor of the old.
PROVERBS 20:29

Someone made me have my picture taken today. I could have refused, but I was in a good mood (note the "was"), so I said I would do it. My husband got out his new digital camera, reread the directions, and in fifteen minutes the photo was on its way from our computer to theirs. Instant ugly.

The problem is, I really had to look at all the pictures to choose the best of the bunch. Usually I look at other things in our pictures—kids, dogs, cat, fish—never at myself. But there I was in close-up, every wrinkle showing, my hair flat, and my smile crooked. I don't deny that's how I usually look to the world—I'm not delusional—but that's not how I think I look. Inside, I'm still somewhere in middle age, so my mental picture is younger than the person in the photo. A lot younger. Thinner, too.

Even worse, I know there's not much chance that things will look better in the next picture. No matter how much I diet or exercise, those wrinkles are there to stay. So it's time to update my mental image, to admit I am the grandmother in the photo and be grateful that I've reached this age. I'm not young anymore, but God still loves me, and so do my family and friends.

If Looks Could Kill: The Green-Eyed Monster

Rachel St. John-Gilbert

"Resentment kills a fool, and envy slays the simple."
JOB 5:2

I only had a "hiyah" relationship with Patty, but I noticed her every time I saw her in our relatively small town. In contrast to us football moms who ran errands in jeans and T-shirts, she was always impeccably dressed in tailored suits—her auburn hair bouncing on her shoulders like a shampoo model. Her makeup was ever fresh, and although she wasn't a classic beauty, Patty had appeal. For Pete's sake, I felt like saying, why can't she, like the rest of us, go to Wal-Mart once in a while looking like something the cat dragged home?

One night after a tough go at putting my kids to bed, then diving right into writing, I looked at the clock and realized it was midnight. It occurred to me that if I didn't run to the store and get some milk, trouble would be brewing alongside my coffee grounds in the morning. Although I've tried, on several milkless occasions, to extol the praises of using orange juice to wet down their cereal, my kids don't buy my "make-do" propaganda.

So, looking like a homeless person—T-shirt dotted with teething biscuit slime, blurred eyeliner the only visible trace of makeup left—I decided to head for the grocery store. My hair was as flat and stringy as Cher's—but the look wasn't as attractive on me as it is on her.

"Ah well," I sighed, heading out the door. "I'll probably be the only customer at this time of night anyway."

At the store, I stared at the paper plate display, trying to decide if I should spring for the cute zoo animal ones, when a woman rolled her cart by me rather hastily. She seemed a bit furtive but offered an obligatory "Hi."

In the split second she passed me, I noticed she wasn't wearing makeup, either, and even had a couple of glowing red zits on her chin. *Good*, I thought, *I'm not the only shameless mommy in this town who is seen in public looking like cat kill.*

And then it hit me. The woman was Perfect Patty. And I thought, *Man! She looks awful! I can't believe she's in public looking like that.* I couldn't have been more pleased. But on the drive home, I wondered, *What does this say about me?* Here I was, looking like I'd hopped off the nearest boxcar, and I'd just pointed the finger at my fellow hobo and declared that my knapsack look was better than hers. Was I envious of Patty's together, hip persona? I think so.

In my heart, I knew that if I got to know Patty, I'd probably find that she was not only nice but that she also struggled with feeling inferior in some area. Then I would be ashamed of myself for envying her. The Bible talks about examining the speck in someone else's eye while we have a log in our own. Or in my case, pointing out the zits on someone else's chin while ignoring the teething biscuit on my own. It's always a good idea to let the scriptures be our "spiritual compact mirror" each day and make sure we are examining our own hearts instead of judging someone else's.

Lookin' Good

Patsy Clairmont

Let us fix our eyes on Jesus, the author and perfecter of our faith.
HEBREWS 12:2

I remember the day well. It was one of those times when everything goes right. I took a shower and fixed my hair. It went just the way I wanted it to, as it so seldom does. I pulled on my new pink sweater, giving me added color, since I need all the help I can get. I pulled on my gray slacks and my taupe heels.

I checked the mirror and thought, *Lookin' good!*

Since it was a cool Michigan day, I slipped on my gray trench coat with pink on the lapels. I was color-coded from head to toe.

When I arrived in downtown Brighton, where I intended to take care of some errands, I was surprised to find heavy traffic. Brighton is a small town, but it has a large health food store. Usually, I can park right in front and run in.

But today business was so brisk I had to park two blocks away. When your attitude is right and it's a great day, however, inconveniences and interruptions are no big deal.

I thought, *I'll just bounce down the street in time to the sunshine.*

I got out of the car, bounced down the street, crossed the road, and entered the store.

As I headed toward the back of the store, I caught my reflection in the glass doors of the refrigeration system. It reaffirmed I was lookin' good. While enjoying my mirrored self, I noticed something was following me. I turned and realized it was my panty hose!

I remembered the night before when I had done a little Wonder Woman act and taken panty hose and slacks off in one fell swoop. This morning I put on my new panty hose and must have pushed the old hose through when I pulled on my slacks.

I believe they made their emergence as I bounced down the street in time to the sunshine. I remembered the truck driver who stopped his truck to let me cross. As I looked up, he was laughing, and I thought, *Oh, look! The whole world is happy today.*

So I waved. Little did I realize how much I was waving.

I assumed I had reached some amount of maturity at this time in my life, but I can honestly say that when I looked back and saw that. . .that. . .dangling participle, the thought that crossed my mind was *I am going to die!*

I knew they were my panty hose because the right foot was securely wrapped around my right ankle. I knew it was secure because I tried to shake the thing off and pretend I had picked it up in the street.

It's amazing to me that we gals buy these things in flat little packages, we wear them once, and they grow. Now I had a mammoth handful of panty hose and no place to pitch them. The shelves were crowded with groceries, and my purse was too small and full, so I stuffed them in my coat pocket. They became a protruding hump on my right hip.

I decided to never leave that store. I knew all the store owners in town, and I figured that by now they would have all their employees at the windows waiting for a return parade.

I glanced cautiously around the store and noticed it was Senior Citizens' day. They were having their blood pressures read, so I got in line to avoid having to leave the store.

The bad news was no one noticed I didn't belong in line. The good news was I had an elevated blood pressure reading. Usually nurses take mine and say, "I'm sorry but you died two days ago." Today I registered well up the scale.

Finally I realized I'd have to leave. I slipped out the door, down the street, into my car, and off for home.

All the way home I said, "I'll never tell anyone I did this, I'll never tell anyone I did this, I'LL NEVER TELL ANYONE I DID THIS!"

I made it home and got out of the car. My husband was in the yard raking.

I screamed, "Do you know what I did?"

He was so proud to know his wife had gone through downtown dragging her underwear. I told him I thought we should move—to another state—in the night. He thought that was extreme and suggested instead that for a while I could walk ten feet behind him. After thinking that through, we decided it should be ten feet in front of him so he could check me out.

If you have ever done anything to embarrass yourself, you know that the more you try not to think about it, the more it comes to you in living color. As I walked through my house, the replay of what I did came to me again and again.

At last I cried out to the Lord, "You take ashes and create beauty, but can You do anything with panty hose?"

Almost immediately I realized that I had dragged a lot worse things through my life than panty hose. I dragged guilt, anger, fear, and shame. I was reminded by the Lord that those were far more unattractive and distracting than my hose, for they prevented others from seeing His presence and His power in my life. I needed to resolve the pain in my past that I might live more fully today and look forward to my tomorrows.

Don't Be Moved!

Michelle Medlock Adams

By the grace given me I say to every one of you: Do not think of yourself more highly than you ought, but rather think of yourself with sober judgment, in accordance with the measure of faith God has given you.
ROMANS 12:3

Singer and actress Britney Spears was voted the sexiest woman in the world by a popular men's magazine in 2004. But in 2005, Spears didn't even make the Top 100 list! She went from being number one to disappearing from the list in one year. Did Spears suddenly lose her sex appeal? Did she lose her loveliness? No, on both counts. As it turns out, the only explanation is this—the world is fickle. People will love you one moment and passionately praise you, and the next moment they may lynch you. Crazy, isn't it?

That's why you can't be moved by what everyone else thinks. This is especially true when it comes to your outward appearance. One day you may get fifteen compliments on your new haircut, and the next day you'll get a zinger something like this: "Wow, you got your hair cut, huh? Don't worry. I had a bad haircut once. It will grow. Lucky for you, hats are in again this season."

Praise is a funny thing. While it's nice to receive, it can

also destroy you if you let it deceive you into thinking too highly of yourself. Beautiful actress, television personality, and singer Jessica Simpson was recently quoted in a *Glamour* cover story as saying: "In this business, you're surrounded by people who praise you all day long. Even at the photo shoot for this cover people kept saying, 'You look so hot.' It's easy to turn into a diva and lose the qualities that made people like you in the first place. And I don't ever want to become that." (Pretty wise words from a person who didn't know if buffalo wings were chicken or if they really came from buffalo!)

So if you rely too heavily on what others think of you—especially what they think of your appearance—you'll never be consistently happy. People change. Their opinions change. But God never changes. He is the same yesterday, today, and forever. And He always thinks you're lovely. After all, He created you in His very likeness. It's like that old expression says, "God made me, and He doesn't make any junk." Hallelujah! Get in the Word of God and discover how God views you. Talk about a self-esteem boost! He adores you, and He always has—even when you wore the "mullet" back in the 1980s.

Don't be moved by praise or criticism. Just go to God and find your identity in Him.

Health

Rx: Chocolate

Martha Bolton

Our mouths were filled with laughter, our tongues with songs of joy.
Psalm 126:2

"Eat your vegetables." That's one sermon we've all heard. Our parents, doctors, nutritionists, and bathroom scales have all been preaching it to us for years, and if we're using our brains, we would follow their advice. It's good advice. Vegetables are healthy (although I think I stand with George Bush on the broccoli controversy).

We've also been told by those in the know that we should be eating seven-grain bread (which, by the way, is only one grain short of pressed board), and we need to be getting our daily supply of calcium (I'm pretty sure Milk Duds don't count).

But that's this week. The rules are always changing. One year this is bad for us. The next year it's good for us and something else is deemed unhealthy.

Take chocolate, for instance. Remember all those candy bars you passed on, those slices of chocolate cake that you waved off at parties? Medical science has now determined that dark chocolate is rich in antioxidants and can actually help protect us against heart disease.

Excuse me? I could have been having chocolate syrup in my Metamucil all these years? Chocolate is *healthy*? Maybe even *healing*? Apparently so. But I'm not surprised. I always knew hot fudge would look great in an IV bag. Just imagine it—chocolate by prescription. Hershey's as a medical deduction on our taxes. Does life get any better than that?

This news could revolutionize the world as we know it. It means Ding Dongs can now be put on the shelf next to the ginseng. It means trick-or-treating could replace going to the gym. And it means Mary See, Sara Lee, and the Keebler elves can all be our personal trainers now.

If chocolate got a bad rap, though, doesn't it make you wonder what other food items they're unjustly keeping away from us? What else have we been told to eat in moderation when it is, in fact, good for us? What if cheesecake is actually a blood thinner? Or tiramisu an antihistamine? What if we can get all the roughage we need from brownies? What if they've been giving us wrong information all these years, making us deny ourselves unnecessarily? Have we been eating bowls of couscous and bean sprouts when all along we could have had Almond Roca? Maybe bran isn't our friend. Maybe it's nougat. Maybe oatmeal causes pimples.

Okay, maybe not. But it is interesting to think about, isn't it? Over a nice, healthy chocolate mocha.

No More Weeds in the Lettuce Salad

Tina Krause

[Jesus said], "The kingdom of heaven is like a man who sowed good seed. . . . But while everyone was sleeping, his enemy came and sowed weeds among the wheat. . . . When the wheat sprouted. . .then the weeds also appeared."
(But not for long; it's time to weed out the weeds.)
MATTHEW 13:24–26

There comes a day in every dieter's life when we'd prefer to toss our low-fat soups and salads into the sea of reckless abandon. I'm at that point now. After weeks of watching what I eat, I want to eat what I watch: whipped cream pies and foods that start with the letter *F*, namely, fried chicken, French fries, and fried veggies served in one of those baskets lined in translucent paper where pools of grease puddle at the bottom.

But tipping the scale at an unmentionable weight has frightened me enough to load my grocery cart with low-fat cottage cheese, crunchy greens, yummy alfalfa sprouts, and soybean everything.

"I mean it, Jim," I announce with the earnestness of a reformed drug addict, "I refuse to eat 'that stuff' again."

"That stuff?"

"Yes, the junk food that turned this once-fit body into a life-size blob of Silly Putty."

Years ago, I was a health enthusiast. I jogged twenty-five miles a week, ate sensibly, and I kept the pounds off for years. Back then, I welcomed seeing people I hadn't talked to in years because I could flaunt my fit physique and bask in the flow of their compliments. Today, I duck behind boxes of Twinkies in the grocery store, hoping no one will notice me.

Of course, I have valid reasons for my weight gain. Here are a few favorites:

- Too little time and too tired to exercise consistently.
- Junk food is quicker and easier to make.
- Stress. (My mantra? When in stress, reach for a plate of double chocolate chip cookies.)
- Middle age. (I always hated the as-you-get-older-it's-harder-to-take-the-weight-off excuse. Now, unlike my clothing, it fits me well.)

Interestingly, my reasons for not doing what I know I should spill over into my spiritual life, too. Though my intentions are good, I allow daily intrusions to rob me from spending time with God. Read my Bible? Maybe later, after I finish my work. Quiet prayer time? I'm just too tired now; I need some sleep.

Excuses pop up faster than weeds after a summer rain.

Sounds similar to a parable Jesus gave when He said that the kingdom of heaven was like a man who sowed good seed, but when everyone slept, the enemy sowed weeds among the wheat. The weeds of sin, worldly preoccupations, and lame excuses choke the seed of God's Word in our hearts. As a result, we become weakened, unproductive, and fruitless.

In moments of weakness, I have ignored the still small voice within. But not anymore.

"Yep, Jim, I'm staying with the program," I say, reinforcing my resolve. "No more excuses."

"What program?" my husband asks from somewhere in oblivion.

"You know, my *diet*?" I snarl. "No more weeds among the lettuce salad for me!"

Confused, my husband exits. But I'm staying with the good seed of God's Word exclusively, even if that includes the alfalfa sprout variety.

WORDS A WOMAN WILL NEVER SAY

"I feel fantastic! I'm retaining water, my stomach is bloated, I have the energy of a garden slug, and in just a few more days it's time for my annual mammogram. Womanhood doesn't get much better than this!"

Bend Me, Shake Me

Debora M. Coty

Heal me, LORD, for my body is in agony.
PSALM 6:2 NLT

Okay, so I was a little tense. Uptight. High-strung as a wet fiddle. Who wouldn't be with two looming book deadlines, a daughter's wedding to plan, and a career change? Even my muscles were sprouting gray hair.

"I know just what you need," my daughter the massage therapist said. "Come to the chiropractor's office where I work, and I'll schedule you for...*The Chair.*"

It was, she explained, a step beyond the relaxing massage chairs I enjoyed when getting an all-too-rare pedicure. "You'll love it, Mom!"

So I naively allowed myself to be strapped into a gray monstrosity secluded behind a curtain, my arms and legs wedged into snugly fitting extensions and my neck scrunched into a slot that forced my head into a crater. It reminded me of another infamous chair, "Old Sparky," the electric chair at the prison where my father worked for twenty-five years.

My trepidation was no less than Old Sparky's last inhabitant as the attendant punched a complex keypad and *The Chair* sprang to life with sounds like whipping helicopter blades. It proceeded to choke my calves, buffet my thighs, knead my bum, and roll steel ball bearings up and down my back like squealing tires on a racetrack.

When I thought I couldn't endure another second, *The Chair* shifted gears and began bucking like a wild bronco. My glasses were knocked askew, my shoes flung off my feet, and my hair teased into a beehive as I was shaken like a throw rug. What power! What whiplash! My taut tendons had no choice but to loosen up or be ripped in half. I felt like Raggedy Ann in a gorilla cage.

Suddenly the rodeo was over. Kong (my nickname for the beast) settled into a relaxing vibration mode, numbing my brain and reducing my muscles to putty in his knobs. Each time my jaw dropped slack enough for a trickle of drool to escape, passing footsteps outside the curtain made me jerk upright, slurp it back in, and try to resume some semblance of dignity in case the shoes entered my cubicle. After the third false alarm, I surrendered my slathering pile of limp flesh to Kong.

But the great ape was only teasing. As if startled by the blast of a hunter's rifle, Kong suddenly roared into action, pounding my now-flaccid flesh like a rump roast being pummeled by a meat mallet.

The attendant who unleashed me took one look at my useless swaying appendages and propped herself against me like a human crutch. My carcass was draped over my steering wheel until I could gather enough strength to turn the ignition key.

This blissful state of physical relaxation is rare for women in our current age of bustling busyness. Stress keeps our muscles tense, minds racing, and spirits restless. Isn't there a better way to find peace than to be battered by a machine?

Yes, dear sister, there is.

"Come to me, all you who are weary and burdened, and I will give you rest" (Matthew 11:28).

Jesus offers peace for our bodies and spirits if we only come to Him. And He's infinitely gentler than Kong!

Fragile Cargo Traveling Home

Tina Krause

Be swift to hear, slow to speak, slow to wrath.
(And eager to follow God's warning signs.)
JAMES 1:19 KJV

There's nothing more nerve-racking than driving a loved one home from the hospital after he or she has undergone major surgery. Fears stumble through your head as you, ever so cautiously, careen away from the hospital entrance with fragile cargo aboard. One tiny fender bender could cause unthinkable consequences to the patient in your care.

Following my husband's spinal surgery, the doctor instructed Jim not to drive or ride in a car for weeks. "Any jarring to the spinal cord could cause permanent paralysis," the doctor warned.

Thank you, Doctor, for this final instruction on the verge of transporting my husband fifty-plus miles through Chicago Loop traffic, rush-hour traffic, local traffic, and then (whew) home.

I can do this, I told myself. *No I can't!* myself snapped back. So my dad, like a kamikaze pilot volunteering for a death mission, sacrificially offered to take the wheel.

Sitting erect, Jim was strapped to the front seat like a

prisoner propped in an electric chair awaiting execution. The bulky neck brace forced his head straight and center. I sat in the backseat directly behind him, slamming my foot on an imaginary brake whenever Dad edged too close to other vehicles.

Meanwhile, I held my breath and vocalized injunctions to drivers who invaded our road space. "Hey there, fella, stay in your own lane! Watch it, wa–a–atch it! Put your turn signal on, lady! Quit huggin' our bumper, mister!"

By the time we arrived home, I was hyperventilating and felt as if I needed an oxygen mask and professional help. As a result, I invented an idea that should be patented— a huge protective bubble covering the car with a sign, required by law, posted on the outside, warning: SLOW-MOVING VEHICLE. HOSPITAL PATIENT TRAVELING HOME. AN AUTOMATIC EXPULSION OF NAILS AND OTHER SHARP OBJECTS WILL DAMAGE ANY CAR THAT COMES WITHIN TEN FEET OF THIS VEHICLE'S ROAD SPACE.

Anything to avoid the unthinkable.

In the same way, imagine if we would consider the consequences of exercising poor judgment, unwise decisions, or thoughtless words before haphazardly stumbling into senseless behavior. What if we guarded our spirit at any cost? I wonder what positive results we'd glean?

The Bible teaches that if we'll obey God's Word, blessings will follow. We carry the precious cargo of a soul and spirit in these timeworn bodies of ours. After the body dies, our spirit travels on, its destination determined by our acceptance or rejection of the gospel of Christ. So it pays to take preventive measures to guard our souls and heed the instructions of the Great Physician. Our life's journey to our final destination is a lot less complicated and a lot more enjoyable that way.

Hmm. How about creating a device to avoid spiritual disaster from encroaching on us? An unseen warning sign written on our hearts declaring: SLOW TO ANGER, SLOW TO SPEAK, CHRISTIAN TRAVELING HOME. EVIL THOUGHTS OR ACTIONS THAT COME WITHIN TEN FEET WILL BE INSTANTLY DEMOLISHED.

Might work. Anything to avoid the unthinkable.

Confidence from Encouraging Others

Ramona Richards

"You yourself have done this plenty of times, spoken words that clarify, encouraged those who were about to quit. Your words have put stumbling people on their feet, put fresh hope in people about to collapse."
JOB 4:3–4 MSG

I don't think I can do this." Elaine sat in the car, refusing to get out. I struggled with what to say, saying a little prayer for guidance. "What are you afraid of?"

She shrugged. "I'm not sure it's fear. More like the embarrassment that makes you clean the house before the maid comes." She paused. "I feel like I should lose weight before joining a gym."

I almost laughed. Elaine had struggled with her weight for years, and here we were, about to go into a gym for the first time in more than twenty years. Elaine, however, now faced her fear of humiliation, in her words, "of being an old fat lady in front of all those young, hard bodies and skinny girls."

It seemed trivial to both of us, given the much larger issues in our lives. But Elaine's fear was real, and it threatened to be crippling, preventing her from making a much-needed change in her life. She needed encouragement; I wanted to offer to her the same help she'd so often given me in the past. It was then that this passage from Job came to mind, when Eliphaz reminded Job that he had so often encouraged his friends in the past, when their doubts had led them away from God. His words had helped them stay on the right path.

"Do you remember," I asked Elaine, "telling me over and over that I'm beautiful in the eyes of God, no matter what people here think?"

She cut her gaze toward me. She didn't want to hear this.

I grinned. "Your advice has always helped me when I had problems thinking straight, especially about God. You are one of the most confident women I know, about everything but this. You told me that confidence lies in God. Yes?"

Reluctantly, Elaine nodded.

"So why is it you think He'll support you with your hardest tasks, but not give you the confidence to do something as simple as walking into a gym?"

We sat in the dark for a long time as Elaine stared out over the parking lot clustered with cars. "I guess," she said finally, "if He can help David and Job through their darkest times, He can help me face a few skinny girls."

We got out, thankful that God could give us the confidence to tackle any task, no matter how big—or small.

Cold but Confident

Tina Krause

*Have no fear. . .for the LORD will be your confidence
and will keep your foot from being snared.*
(My foot, yes, but what about my big mouth?)
PROVERBS 3:25–26

I'm waiting in the doctor's office for my annual exam. Actually, I'm sitting on the edge of the examining table dressed in something that resembles a giant paper napkin. It's cold in here. In fact, it seems the air-conditioning vent is located directly above my head, which explains the frost forming on my neck.

The nurse already took my blood pressure and has escorted me to the scale located in the hallway where any passerby can see what I weigh. I asked—as I always do—if I could take off my shoes and cut my hair before stepping on the scale.

She grinned, and I grimaced as she pushed the weight indicator higher and higher. Aside from breaking into a cold sweat when I saw my real weight—which is always five pounds more than what I weigh at home—I survived.

Barely.

So I've been sitting here, just my napkin and me, for at

least twenty minutes. I know the doctor will appear soon because I heard him entering the examining room next to mine, and I hear muted conversation.

I just want to get this over. Let's see, time to mentally rehearse what I want to say. (I know: I should have written my questions down.) This is nerve-racking. My palms are sweating and my toes are freezing. I think I'm getting sick. I felt fine when I arrived, but I'm certain the man in white will have to prescribe medication for me after I'm finished here.

I hear talking in the hall. Sounds like the doctor. I brace myself. Nope, he walked away. Now I'm really nervous. I'm getting a headache and I just sneezed. Great. I can't even think straight. Why am I here anyway? I've forgotten.

Fear and intimidation strike every time I visit the doctor. Most women are acquainted with these haunting emotions. Whether in a physical exam, a final exam, or on an important project, a lack of confidence thrusts us into a whirlwind of insecurity and inferiority. For no apparent reason, otherwise confident, stable women are reduced to precarious behavior as their thoughts run amok.

But when intimidation strikes and our insecurities surface, God assures us we have no reason to fear. We can rely upon Him to restore our confidence when ours evaporates in the winds of uncertainty.

Uh-oh, I hear rustling outside the examining room door. I think this is it. The door is opening. *Lord, please help me.*

"Hi, Tina. How are you?"

"Oh, fine." Hmm, suddenly I feel pretty good.

"What seems to be the problem?"

"Well to be honest, Doc, it's this paper napkin and that air-conditioning system of yours. And why must I be publicly weighed every time I walk through the door to this place?"

Oops, perhaps a smaller dose of confidence would do.

WORDS A WOMAN WILL NEVER SAY

"Eating celery sticks and low-fat cottage cheese for the rest of my life is the ultimate thrill. But since I prefer the plus-size look, I guess I'll have to settle for peanut butter parfaits, fettuccini Alfredo, and double-cheese sausage pizzas."

Confessions of a Chocoholic

Dena Dyer

"Life is more than food, and the body more than clothes."
LUKE 12:23

I love to eat; I always have. Chocolate? Yum. Salsa and cheese dip? Love 'em! Italian food? Gimme some!

When I was younger, my body accepted my sometimes-poor eating habits with no adverse side effects. But as I stopped growing in height, I started growing in girth. In fact, each time my life changed in a dramatic way, I put on weight.

First, there was the freshman fifteen. Then I put on the newlywed twenty, and later, the new baby thirty. By that time—my late twenties—I realized something had to change. So I began to diet.

And believe me, I tried them all. But Slim-Fast made me gag, a low-carb diet made me crazy, and Weight Watchers made me hungry. I even tried a plan that had its followers ingesting one kind of food all day, and then switching. For example, one day was grapes, the next pineapple—and I hate pineapple! It was supposed to burn fat, but it just burned me out.

The South Beach Diet was working well for me until I got pregnant and had to stop doing it. (Now I'm thinking about creating a "Nude Beach Diet." You observe—fully clothed, of course, a nude beach. Then you either feel great about your body and don't want to diet anymore, or you have the motivation to never eat again. Could be quite popular, don't you think?)

But I finally came to the conclusion that unless I wanted to look like a Macy's Thanksgiving Day parade balloon by the time I was forty, I had to make a lifestyle change. That meant I was going to have to alter my habits and let God give me some discipline (uh-oh!). God also challenged me to start looking to Him to meet some of the needs I was filling through unhealthy eating patterns.

So I started to exercise regularly and began to choose smaller portions and healthy alternatives at stores and restaurants. And you know what? It worked. I'm still not model-thin, by any means. I never will be, and most days, I'm okay with that. But I feel much better—physically and spiritually.

Throughout my struggle with weight, God has reminded me time and again that He wants to be my food. Some days I let Him fill me up with His peace and power, and other days I run (again!) to the candy machine.

I've learned that my spiritual life is a lot like my eating habits. It's a daily battle to let Jesus, the Bread of Life, be my sustenance. It's much easier to run to the television, read a gossip magazine, or call a friend than it is to take the time to tell God what's bothering me and let Him work on my problems.

So my earnest prayer has become, "Lord Jesus, help me to hunger for You more than I hunger for earthly food. Make me as excited about spending time with You as I am about going out to eat."

And sometimes I add this postscript: "One more thing, Lord—please let there be chocolate in heaven."

The Giddies

Tina Krause

*LORD, make me to know mine end, and the measure of my days. . .
that I may know how frail I am.* (And should I forget. . .
give me a case of the giddies to keep me in check.)
PSALM 39:4 KJV

Single file, I followed the other choir members to the choir loft. The organ accompanied our procession, robes swaying with each step. Church was about to begin, so I put forth an effort to look my Sunday best.

But I had one problem. Before the service, another choir member and I had engaged in some lighthearted jesting. Now we had a serious case of the giddies. Everything struck a humorous chord—the pastor's slight hop to the platform, the choir director's mannerisms, and the child squirming in the front pew.

Facing the congregation, I tried to restrain my laughter as my face flushed and tears formed. Church members peered over the tops of their hymnals looking at me. For a moment I was fine until I noticed a fly land on Mrs. Baker's head. She swatted the pest; then it landed on her face. She flinched and shooed it away, but it landed again. Her eyebrows furrowed as she stared at the pest, waiting for it to take flight. When it did, she waved her hands like a flagman at an Indy 500 race.

Instantly, my shoulders shook as laughter bubbled within like a volcano about to erupt. My friend alongside of me put her hand over her mouth and stared at the floor. Meanwhile, I prayed that I could gain control.

All eyes were on the front. *Quick, think sad thoughts,* I told myself in desperation—anything to cure the giggles. But nothing worked. The minister's mispronunciation of a name set me off again as waves of unrestrained chuckles rippled from my mouth.

Finally, the worst—an unexpected snort. Eyebrows lifted with frowns of disapproval. I wanted to disappear. *How could I allow myself to get so out of control? What must everyone think? What must the pastor think? What must* God *think?*

In an instant, the giddies vanished while humiliation and embarrassment gripped me like two giant bear claws. I bowed my head, my face now flushed for a different reason.

To my relief, the pastor whisked around and quipped, "If a merry heart works like a medicine as the scriptures say, someone in the choir is the healthiest person in here!"

Laughter filled the sanctuary and I was comforted. My pastor's gracious lightheartedness rescued me.

Most of us go to church dressed in our Sunday clothes and Sunday smiles. We want folks to applaud our spirituality. But occasionally something occurs to expose what we really are: human.

When our human frailties break through in waves of the ridiculous, God's mercy prevails. After all, to be human isn't a sin, but to pretend we're not is really something to laugh about!

Root for Me: When in Pain, Ask for Help

Rachel St. John-Gilbert

"Ask and it will be given to you; seek and you will find;
knock and the door will be opened to you."
MATTHEW 7:7

My visit with my sister at her timeshare had been relaxing and refreshing. The moonlight on the lake below promised a lifetime of tranquility. I sipped from a piping hot mug of green tea and prepared to let out a great sigh: "Ah–h–h–h. . ." What came out of my mouth instead was a wrenching "Argh–h–h!" My right back molar suddenly felt like a miniature volcano, preparing to explode.

"Musta been the tea," I muttered and headed for bed, hoping the throbbing would subside. By 3 a.m., my tooth had developed the attitude of a cranky New York cabbie.

"Hey!" I could almost hear it. "I'm dyin' he–yah! Can I get some drugs, or what?" I scurried to the bathroom and rifled through my overnight bag. I could only find a sample bottle of infant pain reliever. I unscrewed the top of the one-inch-tall bottle and guzzled the contents like a two-bit junkie—New York style. Dragging back to bed, my gaze fell on my teething six-month-old, sleeping peacefully in her port-a-crib.

"Sorry, kid," I whispered apologetically.

After a few more pain-filled days and fitful nights, my toothache morphed into jaw spasm, of all things! It equaled any pain I had ever experienced in childbirth.

What's going on? I wondered as I tried to massage my muscles into submission. *Is it stress? TMJ? What if I have to live with chronic pain for the rest of my life?* My mind raced and my mood deteriorated, while my jaws clenched tighter.

I finally called an acquaintance who was a dentist. "Might be an abscessed tooth," she said. "Call my husband at his oral surgery office. See what he says."

Dr. Pollack examined my jaws and ruled out TMJ. "You should see an endodontist right away," he advised, "but meanwhile, I'm going to give you some strong drugs."

While he wrote the prescription, I sat there looking like Lizard Woman—bulging eyes red and swollen half shut from sleep deprivation and crying.

After a deliciously restful night of sleep (go drugs!), I went to see the endodontist, Dr. Rakusin. He was a native of South Africa with a lilting accent and soothing voice—a definite plus for someone who is about to yank the roots out from under your tooth. The good doctor, who quickly determined that he faced the equivalent of an agitated Sasquatch, wasted no time getting to the numbing process.

"You will feel a pinch," he said softly, as he guided the silver syringe to the roof of my aching mouth. "This might be a little uncomfortable," he added as he poked another spot. I was nervous, but as the pain subsided, I relaxed. For the first time in several days, I felt my lizardness melting away as vestiges of my former self returned.

Then I heard a whir, a clink, and a whiz, and. . .it was over. "That's it?" I asked, incredulous yet grateful.

"That's it!" responded Super Endodontist Man. As he turned to put away his tools, his white coat flung open, and I'm certain I saw a giant *E* emblazoned across his chest. My hee–ro.

In a subsequent visit, the kind doctor dubbed me the endodontist's evangelist. Guilty as charged, I found myself talking to anyone within earshot about the joys of root canals. I was the latter-day Lazarus of dental patients, risen from the abyss of abscess.

When we're hurting, it's easy for our mood to escalate from troubled to traumatized. If you're going through a tough time emotionally, physically, or spiritually, don't wait for your situation to go from bad to worse. Seek help and encouragement early—whether from a friend or a professional. You may be surprised at how simple (or relatively painless!) the solution might be or how much better you will feel by seeking solace.

Buoyancy Is a Wonderful Asset

Tina Krause

*Does not the potter [God] have the right to make out of the same lump
of clay some pottery for noble purposes and some for common use?*
(And some for floating and some for sinking?)
ROMANS 9:21

Even in my slim-and-trim days, I stored enough body fat
to bob like a cork whenever I touched water.

At first my buoyancy was a wonderful asset. Floating
backside with arms and legs outstretched, I'd stare up at the
summer sky as if reclined on a La-Z-Boy. Admiring my gift
of levity, my husband and two sons watched in awe.

"Man, it's like Mom can float forever," son Jimmy
observed. Afterward, I'd instruct the threesome on my floating techniques, but lacking adequate adipose to stay afloat for
more than five seconds, each one sank the moment I released
hold of them.

Soon, instead of admiration, I inspired vacation family
fun. My buoyancy provided more laughter than a slapstick
comedy as we routinely beelined for the hotel pool to devise
water games.

"Let's toss a quarter to the bottom of the pool and see
who gets it first," son Jeff suggested. As we plunged into

the water, Dad and boys sank with brick consistency, while I struggled to lunge deep enough to reach the bottom of the pool. Hysterical with laughter, my husband shot to the surface to grab my arm and pull me down, providing leverage. Meanwhile, the kids paddled to the bottom, leaving behind a stream of bubbles from their underwater guffaws.

Nevertheless, I boasted one award-winning game: Who could tread water the longest? "Hey, that's no fair!" Jimmy protested at the mere mention of the game as his brother Jeff chimed in. "Yeah, we all know Mom is unsinkable!"

After the jesting subsided, my husband, the voice of sensitivity and compassion, soothed me with his trademark brand of consolation. "Look on the positive side, honey," he said, concealing a grin. "Your built-in life preserver might come in handy someday. I mean, think of how many people you could have saved on the *Titanic*."

I leveled a stern scowl in his direction. "Yeah, that's right, just throw my body overboard and instruct people to latch on!"

Perhaps my heartless husband had a point, though. God views us much differently than we view ourselves; He sees the possibilities beneath our flaws. Our imperfections serve as stepping-stones for God to work in our lives. Rather than dwelling on the negatives, the Lord maximizes our lives to their fullest potential, despite our apparent flaws.

With that in mind, I choose to consider my buoyancy as a positive trait. After all, for a woman who fears scales more than she fears the dentist's drill, treading water is the only time I actually experience weightlessness. No matter how much body fat accumulates, I'm a featherweight in water, and life is smooth sailing. . .I mean, floating.

And hey, let's not underestimate my unique life-saving capabilities!

WORDS A WOMAN WILL NEVER SAY

"A day at the beach is an exhilarating event. Donned in my sleeveless muumuu, I sit on a beach blanket and wave to passersby while the ocean waves ripple in cadence with my flabby upper arms."

Cookie Caper

Patsy Clairmont

No temptation has seized you except what is common to man.
1 CORINTHIANS 10:13

White creamy clouds of marshmallow atop a thin layer of graham cracker, covered and sealed in a smooth two-inch tower of chocolate—the lick-your-fingers-and-catch-the-crumbs kind of cookies.

I have this "thing" for chocolate marshmallow cookies—alias pinwheels. At first I didn't realize I had a thing. I told myself I was only buying them for my family. But when I began to resent sharing those sweet treats with my husband and our boys, I took a closer look at my cookie consumption.

In a let's-get-healthy moment, I decided to give up my prized pinwheels. The problem was, one cookie was left and, well, I sort of thought it would be wasteful to throw it out.

Besides I'm not too good at this denial stuff—at least not cold cookie. But to eat the last cookie right then seemed so. . . so sudden.

Plus, when you know this is your last cookie, you don't want to just devour it. The moment should be more ceremonial. The cookie needs to be savored. It needs to be appreciated. It needs to be mine! And I knew if I did a couple of household tasks, which I should do, I wouldn't feel as bad when I ate the last cookie, which I shouldn't do.

To protect my piggish plan, I went into the kitchen and hid the cookie from my family. I tucked it in the bottom kitchen drawer behind the rolling pin, next to the measuring cups, with two hot pads carefully placed over the top to form a roof for my little sugar shack. Then I quietly slid closed the drawer and headed off to do my chores.

I cleaned my desk, dusted the living room, and changed the sheets on the boys' beds. Then I headed for the kitchen, feeling I had earned this moment.

I checked over both shoulders before sliding open the drawer and removing the roof. There was the rolling pin and the measuring cups. And next to them was. . .the spot where the cookie should have been. My cookie was gone!

The next thing I remember I was running through the house, grabbing my purse and keys, and crying out, "But, Lord, I said just one more cookie!"

I sprinted to my car and hightailed it for the grocery store. I heard myself murmuring, "Just one more cookie, just one more cookie."

Finally I was in the store, moving quickly, far too quickly I realize now as I think back on the little children I had to move aside to clear the way to the cookie aisle.

At last! I had arrived and there, where they should be, were the cookies. Only one bag of pinwheels was left.

As I stood there, faced with my vice, that package packed with chocolate, I reminded myself I was an adult, and I had a choice to make. I could buy them, or I could turn and walk away a wiser woman.

Well, I ate two on the way to the checkout lane and three more on the way home.

By the time I pulled into the driveway I was full, and it wasn't just from the cookies. It was also the guilt. I was mad at myself. To think a grown woman could be controlled by a two-inch glob of chocolate!

I thought I was more mature than that. Funny, the Lord didn't seem surprised at all.

WORDS A WOMAN WILL NEVER SAY

"Don't tell me I need more sweets in my diet. I'm aware of that and I'm trying my best to eat more. Just give me time. It takes discipline to achieve such a lofty goal."

For All You Sugar Junkies

Tina Krause

*"Blessed are those who hunger and thirst for righteousness,
for they will be filled."* (And never crave junk food again.)
MATTHEW 5:6

I've noticed something interesting about myself. The only solicitors I welcome to my door are schoolchildren toting cardboard boxes filled with candy.

Now why is that? Is it because I'm sympathetic toward the little darlings? Ah, no. Is it because I'm a mother and understand the importance of fund-raising? Afraid not. Rather, my benevolence stems from something more self-indulgent, namely, my sweetaholic tendencies.

That's right, I admit it. I relish the instant gratification I receive whenever one of those giant-size chocolate candy bars appeases my sugar cravings. What's more, I like it even better when obtaining my fix takes little or no effort on my part.

But I'm not alone. At the office I've seen entire boxes of candy wiped out in a matter of hours. In fact, one way to increase your child's candy sales is to take a full box with you to your place of employment. It's a sure sell.

Gift wrap, candles, and all-occasion cards don't have the same persuasive marketing capabilities that candy does.

Why? Because sweetaholics are in the majority, and we will do just about anything to satisfy our cravings.

One sure sign of a sugar junkie is her willingness to buy. Most times, it is unnecessary to approach a sweetaholic to make a sale. We're the ones who exclaim, "Oh good! You still have a few peanut butter cups left!" as we cheerfully dish out another two dollars before the person holding the box of candy can so much as open his or her little mouth.

What's the big attraction anyway? Candy is junk. It's loaded with empty calories and has zero nutritional value; yet our uncontrollable cravings for it drive us to obsessive behavior.

Yesterday a student came to my door selling candy for a school fund-raiser. I was thrilled. I bolted up the stairs to search for money while the schoolgirl stood outside my door. The inside of my purse looked like a war zone as I frantically scrambled through it for signs of loose change. Gathering a handful of coins, I dashed downstairs, eager to pay the child, grab the candy, and head for the nearest chair to savor my M&Ms.

That's when it occurred to me: When was the last time I bolted up the stairs, grabbed my Bible, and headed for the nearest chair to savor the food of God's Word?

The Bible tells us to "Taste and see that the Lord is good" (Psalm 34:8). That first "taste" comes when we choose to feast at the table of God's Word; unlike the junk food of life, Jesus satisfies. The Bible is the spiritual food by which we grow; it contains the life-sustaining meat and potatoes we all require. It is packed with nutrients that provide salvation for our souls, strength for our spirits, renewal for our minds, and hope for our futures. To those who ingest its life-giving words, the scriptures provide strength and restoration. So why do I opt for the junk foods of life instead?

Oops, excuse me a minute, someone else is at my door. "You're selling chocolate what? Ah, no thanks. I'm a meat-and-potato person myself."

Exercise

Weight for Me

Rachel St. John-Gilbert

I can do everything through him who gives me strength.
PHILIPPIANS 4:13

For years I noted, though with a sense of detachment, that many people over the age of forty joke about developing a "spare tire." Midsection weight never concerned me because I was born a "perfect pear"—you know, with hips and a waistline, but not much tummy. But that changed when I turned forty-two.

I would like to say that I didn't see it coming or do anything to cause it. But the truth is that I overate and under-exercised all that summer, and when it was time to come out of the pool and face the fall, I ended up with the equivalent of an inflatable swim ring permanently encircling my waist.

"How can this happen to me?" I asked the plump stranger in my mirror. "I'm a *pear* for Pete's sake! How can I be an apple *and* a pear? I'm beginning to look like those guys in the Fruit of the Loom underwear commercials. What's next? A perfect pineapple?"

I tried reasoning with the middle-aged (yikes! I've said it!) smartie in the mirror.

"That little bitty swim ring isn't *that* noticeable. It's more like a smallish pork tenderloin round my middle." I set about to make the statement true by frantically searching in my closet for longer and fuller blouses. None of them was as cute as I'd remembered. Maybe I'd try something a little—well, younger. Off I went shopping and wouldn't you know, I soon noticed a woman about my age who was wearing a short-waisted, teenybopper top. The space between the bottom of her top and the top of her bottom looked like a giant muffin whose "batter" had oozed over the edges. Sighing, I turned back to the women's department.

There seemed to be only one way out, and you probably already know what it was: the much avoided diet and exercise plan. So, for the first time since I was a slightly chubby preteen and a card-carrying member of Weight Watchers, I enrolled in a weight-loss program. I had joined Weight Watchers so many times over the years they probably had a wing named after me at headquarters, but somehow I told myself this plan would be different. Gradually I'm learning to eat meals the "size of my loosely clenched fist" (chicken the size of my cell phone, salmon the size of my son's iPod) and chewing *tediously* slowly.

In weaker moments, I want to take my loosely clenched fist and wrap it, oh so lovingly, around a nice waffle cone filled with rocky-road ice cream smothered with hot fudge sauce and toasted pecans. Or I yearn for an eclair the size of my cell phone and iPod combined. At my detestable weakest, I'd like to wrap my tightly clinched fist around the instructor's neck and ask *tediously* slowly, "How would you like a breath of air the size of my fist?"

However, in my stronger moments, I'm learning real advantages in cutting my PB&J sandwich into four sections and chewing each bite like a cow chewing her cud, rather than stuffing it down while standing over the sink. The process is at least slowing down my intake, which helps me *look* less like a cow.

I've also realized that during my meals, I often stop and take the time to watch my little chicks playing happily in the sandbox, to notice the butterflies alighting on my red tulips, and other wonders of my surroundings. Hey! There are other things in life besides food! I missed these delights when I grazed at the speed of a wood-chipping machine.

Practically speaking, this slow-down technique is designed to help my tummy tell my brain, "Excuse me, but I'm about to bust down here!" Theoretically this practice will keep me from tossing extra helpings down my gullet willy-nilly, thus deflating the built-in swim ring around my external middle.

Undoing a lifetime of unhealthy eating patterns is daunting and exhausting. Having to undo a lifetime of *anything* is exhausting. Some days I'm tempted to beat myself up and think *I'm such a loser. . .*or in this case such a *gainer*!

On other days, I'm encouraged that I'm learning a new way of being that might finally deflate my spare tire, jelly mold, floatie ring, love handles—whatever.

Yes, good things are happening. Somewhere between

near-starvation and grunts of agony during exercise, I learned that renewing my figure is very much tied to renewing my mind. Jesus loves me, this I know. I'm not alone in the battle of the bulge.

WORDS A WOMAN WILL NEVER SAY

"All right. I apologize for flaunting my dimpled thighs. But I thought their craterlike formations were really artistic, and before I knew it, pride got the best of me."

Brain Workouts

Martha Bolton

Rejoice in the Lord always. I will say it again: Rejoice!
PHILIPPIANS 4:4

Exercise is supposed to be good for the mind. If that's true, then brain exercises must really be healthy. No, I'm not talking about solving brainteasers, doing crossword puzzles, taking IQ tests, or anything like that. I'm talking about exercises *in* the brain. In other words, doing push-ups and sit-ups, jogging, cross-country skiing, weight lifting, even Iditarod racing, but doing it all in my head.

You see, I'm convinced that dreaming about exercising has almost as many health benefits as the actual exercise itself. If you don't agree, the next time you're running from that crazed maniac in your sleep, force yourself awake and then take your pulse. If my theory is correct, it'll be racing, your heart will be pounding, and you'll be so wet with sweat you'll feel like you just participated in a triathlon in Alabama in the middle of July! That's the power of the mind. It can make your body think that it's actually going through whatever it is that your mind is imagining.

It stands to reason then, that thinking about physical exercise must do us some good, right?

All right, my doctor didn't buy it either. For some reason, he's of the opinion that my exercise program needs to take place during my waking hours to do me any good.

But doesn't he realize I could hurt myself exercising? Not only can I accidentally slap myself silly during a round of jumping jacks, but I almost broke a hip once on a treadmill when my pillow got stuck on the conveyor belt and knocked me off onto the floor.

Giving his advice the benefit of the doubt, however, I've decided to look into the possibility of getting a personal trainer to help get me in shape. So far I haven't found one I like, though. None of them will allow me to hang Krispy Kreme doughnuts off the barbells to give me an incentive for lifting weights. (If you know one who offers this as part of his workout plan, I am taking referrals.)

Aerobics would be all right if they'd slow down the pace a little. I don't mind working out to the golden oldies, but there's a world of difference between exercising to "The Boogie Woogie Bugle Boy" and "Gentle on My Mind." I prefer the latter.

I did give tennis some thought. After all, most tennis players look like they're in pretty good shape. But tennis seems like a lot of work for nothing. All the players do is hit the ball back and forth and forth and back. How much fun could that be? And then there's all that running trying to dodge the ball. If you ask me, the only good thing about tennis is that the net comes in handy as a hammock.

That's why I maintain that brain exercises are the best.

With brain exercises you're your own personal trainer and you're in total control. In your mind you never have to wait in line to use the Nautilus equipment, you always look great in your bathing suit while swimming those laps, and there's very little risk of any physical injury. (Unless, of course, you sleepwalk. In which case I'd keep the bathtub filled with water. A high dive from the sink into an empty tub could really hurt.)

In this day of limited free time, I think brain exercising is a concept that might really catch on. And we don't have to stop with just exercising. I also have been known to have brain concerts (Celine Dion has nothing on me), give brain speeches (a standing ovation every time), and go brain skydiving (haven't landed in a tree yet), and I've even run for president in my head. (I don't know if I won yet, though. We're still counting the hanging chads.)

Bird of Pray: God in Unexpected Places

Rachel St. John-Gilbert

Every good and perfect gift is from above,
coming down from the Father.
JAMES 1:17

When I was a young single gal with a robust appetite and a lean dating life, I decided to take up running to prevent certain body parts from spreading. I wanted to enhance both my body and my odds for meeting Mr. Right. But the way things were going, I was well on my way to becoming the next Mrs. Jack Sprat. It was clearly time to spring into action.

I had just moved to Virginia, and my running routes wound through gorgeous tree-lined neighborhoods with pines that reached to the sky. The sun flickered through those tall branches, and I felt close to heaven whenever I gazed upward, letting the rays drench my face with their warmth.

On one particularly beautiful spring morning, hundreds of pink and white azalea bushes were in breathtaking bloom. I felt as if I were jogging through a dense, colorful wonderland of cotton candy.

I was so overtaken by the sheer glory of the moment, I began to sing: "Praise God from whom all blessings flow, praise Him all creatures. . ." I belted out every word, my heart soaring. Just as I was feeling rather Snow Whitey and about to exhort the woodland creatures to chime in, I felt a thump on my shoulder. I stopped to make sure I hadn't been shot with a BB gun by a naughty neighborhood hooligan.

Instead, I noticed approximately two tablespoons of white, green-flecked gunk oozing down my shoulder, staining my brand-new running shirt. This was not the thanks I expected from the Lord of Creation upon breaking into song for Him. Cautiously, I glanced skyward to see an egret gracefully (now that he had lightened his load) gliding through the sunlit sky. I began to laugh. "God," I prayed, "You sure have a weird sense of humor."

I don't know about you, but occasionally I feel God doesn't respond to me in quite the way I expect. During that fateful jog, I was innocently expressing my gratitude to Him for life and, ironically, for nature. And what did I get? Bird poop on my shoulder. And I was irritated with God for a nanosecond.

But I also got a reminder that God often uses humor to show me He's a real Person with a full range of emotions— and I felt closer to Him for having made me laugh. And I also got the message that the Creator can rain down all kinds of things from heaven to get His children's attention and prompt their prayers and praise.

Animals

God's Delight in His Creation

Marilyn Meberg

"In this world you will have trouble.
But take heart! I have overcome the world."
JOHN 16:33

I'm filled with the wonder and cheer at the thought of how delightfully God has created penguins. They charm me and inspire me spiritually. They are waddling little overcomers who, because of a God-created system, survive earth's harshest environment, living out their quirky lives with efficiency as well as organization. What's the source of their overcoming abilities? God. Plain, simple, and profound.

I love that Jesus made references to the birds of the air and the flowers of the field as objects of His loving care. In the divine mind, all creation is valued and provided for. In fact, Jesus even suggested we look to nature to note creation's God-given ability to function, perform, and overcome, and then to be encouraged and cheered that His commitment to meeting our needs is even greater. What is equally inspiring to me is that God take obvious delight in His creation. (You have to admit, hatching an egg on the toe of a penguin is zany!)

God's delight in us is expressed frequently in scripture.

For example, Psalm 18:19 states, "He brought me out into a spacious place; he rescued me because he delighted in me." It's mind-boggling to most of us that the God of the universe actually delights in us, but scripture says He does.

If John 16:33 is a divine formula for cheerful living, we see that Jesus warned us we would experience bad stuff as long as we were on the earth. But in spite of all that, He says we can be cheerful because He has "overcome the world." The understanding of that last phase is crucial to finding cheer in the midst of the "stuff." I think we first have to underscore the tremendous love and delight God feels for us before we even begin to grasp the magnitude of what He overcame on the cross. His love sent Jesus to the cross; knowing He delights in us allows us to feel secure about who we are and whose we are.

We can't find cheer if we don't know Jesus as Savior. But when we do know Him, by virtue of His Spirit being linked to ours, we have access to His overcoming power for absolutely every trial that touches our lives.

To find cheer, we also must internalize the vast depth of God's love. How few of us really grasp that truth. We talk it, we quote it, we remind each other about it, but do we know it? I'll have to say in all candor, I struggle daily with my inability to comprehend God's boundless, unconditional, and even relentless love for me.

However, I don't think it's possible to be a cheerful overcomer without the sure foundation of knowing God loves me exactly as I am once I have received forgiveness for sin. I can't do anything to win Him, impress Him, or further convince Him I am worthy of His love and delight. That has already been done. Jesus did that on the cross. He made me perfectly and wholly acceptable to God.

Moose

Toni Sortor

*God made the wild animals according to their kinds, the livestock. . .
and all the creatures that move along the ground according
to their kinds. And God saw that it was good.*
GENESIS 1:25

I know that God has a sense of humor. He did, after all, create the moose, which looks like a horse gone incredibly wrong. I met my first moose in the middle of an isolated logging road. We made the mistake of rounding a blind bend a little too fast, coming face-to-knee with a young animal who stood his ground in true moose fashion. My first thought was, *He's so big!* Television or photographs do not convey the sheer massiveness of a moose—even a young one.

Moose are not overly intelligent. Fortunately, they are exceedingly calm, collected animals, curious and patient with humans who invade their space. They look us over and usually decide we're no threat—not a wise decision during hunting season. This particular moose blocked the road for a good ten minutes to look us over before ambling off into the bushes on moose business.

No human who has ever shared space with a moose can avoid loving them. Their ugliness, their bony long legs, their cowlike eyes—you just can't resist them, even though you know they can do fatal damage if they collide with a car. They are somewhat like an ugly baby—always a surprise, but one that makes you smile in spite of yourself and thank God for providing such unexpected delight. God didn't make the moose beautiful or smart, just irresistible, and seeing a moose can only be considered a blessing.

Bulldog Faith

Michelle Medlock Adams

And he did not do many miracles there because of their lack of faith.
MATTHEW 13:58

Have you ever heard the theory that people end up owning the dog breed that they most resemble in the looks department? Well, I'd have to say that is true when it comes to me. I am the proud "mama" to three long-haired miniature dachshunds. They have long noses and very short legs. Yeah, I would have to say that I share those same figure flaws. (You're checking out your dog right now, aren't you?)

But in the spiritual realm, we all need to resemble English bulldogs. Bible teacher Kate McVeigh once shared that Christians need to have bulldog faith. She said, "A bulldog only knows one thing. That bone is his, and he's taking it." And that bulldog won't let loose of that bone—no matter what. In fact, the English bulldog's jaw muscles are as strong as any athlete's muscle, and when it latches on to something, it really latches on.

Well, guess what? That's how we have to be when it comes to our faith. In Mark 11:23–24, Jesus says, "I tell you the truth, if anyone says to this mountain, 'Go, throw yourself into the sea,' and does not doubt in his heart but believes that what he says will happen, it will be done for him. Therefore I tell you, whatever you ask for in prayer, believe that you have received it, and it will be yours."

In other words, you have to believe you have received your deliverance from drugs. You have to believe you have received your healing. You have to believe you've received a restored marriage. You have to believe that you've received your dream job. And then you can't be moved if it doesn't happen overnight. You have to get a locked jaw of faith on whatever it is you're trusting God to do in your life, and you can't turn loose until the desired result comes. So go ahead. Growl in the face of adversity and develop that bulldog faith. It may be a dog-eat-dog world out there, but with bulldog faith, you'll have a beautiful existence.

The Vet's

Toni Sortor

Do not despise the LORD's discipline and do not resent his rebuke, because the LORD disciplines those he loves.
PROVERBS 3:11–12

One of the cats has to go to the vet's today. She just had her checkup; then we went back to get the flea medicine, and now her ears are itching. I wouldn't mind all this so much if it didn't involve getting her into and out of the cat carrier. Doing so requires qualities only found in the Special Forces: infiltration, encirclement, and neutralization. Then there's the effort required to fold four rigid, outspread legs down into the carrier at one time without losing your grip on the cat's body or being seriously scratched.

Cats are not stupid. They must know this is all for their benefit, that they will no longer itch or hurt when it's over and we bring them home in about ten minutes. But they still fight it. They act as if we are trying to kill them when we are actually saving them.

Of course, I'm no better when God decides I am in need of correction or remedy. I fight it every time He tries to get a hold on me and put me where I need to be. I don't want to go—the carrier is small and frightening—so I make corralling me as difficult as possible. Fortunately, God is far more patient than we are with the cats and doesn't use brute force on us. As with the cats when it's time to go home, all He does is leave the door open, and I walk right in.

Work

Walk in Love

Michelle Medlock Adams

Love is kind.
1 CORINTHIANS 13:4

"Happy birthday, Michelle!" shouted three of my closest coworkers. They had decorated my office and sprinkled it with fun-sized chocolate candy bars. They knew I'd need an extra lift. After all, it was my thirtieth birthday. I had been dreading it for weeks. Leaving behind my twenties was a tough one. I feared that crow's-feet were just around the corner. But my buddies were there to cheer me up—except for Claire.

As I headed downstairs for my morning Diet Coke, she stopped me in the hallway. "So how old are you today?"

"I'm thirty," I whispered.

"Really?" Claire said, raising her eyebrows. "I thought you were *way* older than that."

With that curt comment, she took her size-four body down the hall, leaving me feeling deflated and miserable. She was great at spewing hurtful comments on a daily basis. Oh, how I longed to say some zingers back at her. I had crafted them carefully in my mind, just waiting for the right time. But whenever that opportunity arose, the Lord wouldn't let me speak. I kept hearing that inner voice saying, "Walk in love."

Maybe there's a "Claire" in your office that you'd like to throttle. Well, don't. Instead, kill her with kindness. Walk in love. Yes, it's difficult, but you don't have to walk it alone. God will help you.

Tightening Those Loose Lips

Debora M. Coty

We all make many mistakes, but those who control their tongues can also control themselves in every other way.
JAMES 3:2 NLT

It was a hectic morning at my job as an occupational therapist in a rehabilitation facility. I was evaluating a new stroke patient—a thirty-something single man—who was working up a sweat on the upper extremity bicycle.

Using my most professional tone, I began to instruct him to take a break, but at the last second decided to substitute, "Take a rest." To my horror, out of my mouth came, "Just stop a minute and take a breast."

As my shocking faux pas hung in the air, we stared at each other for a long moment. He blinked. Twice. Then one eyebrow shot up and a smile tugged at his mouth as he turned to the woman sitting next to him and exclaimed with bright eyes, "I think I'm going to like therapy!"

I'm not one to let thoughts marinate long before spewing them out of my mouth. In fact, I've been told that I live my life out loud. Like a foghorn. Psalm 39:1 should be bolted to my forehead: "I will guard my mouth as with a muzzle" (NASB).

Once while I was walking my dog, the boy next door buzzed his electronic scooter right up behind us on the sidewalk, driving my dog wild. Annoyance overrode neighborliness. "Not too bright, are you, son?" I shouted over the din and turned to find his red-faced mother standing in her doorway.

In the grocery store checkout line, I loudly announced how *rude* the woman behind me was for barging her buggy in front of mine when a new lane opened. And then I suddenly realized she was the mother of one of my Sunday school students.

Loose lips moments can be horrible. . .or horribly funny.

Like the minister who was preaching a scathing sermon about sin within his flock and wasn't aware his fly was open. As his teenage son tried to clue him in by a "zip the lips" gesture from the back row, the indignant pastor responded, "I know some of you will try to get me to zip it up, but I'm not doing it!"

Or my friend Rhonda who inadvertently dropped a "t" in her church presentation about eternal life and proclaimed to her audience, "God wants you to live forever in *immorality*."

God's word has plenty to say about loose lips. Psalm 34:13 admonishes us to "Keep your tongue from evil." James 3:5 reminds us, "The tongue is a small thing, but what enormous damage it can do. A tiny spark can set a great forest on fire" (NLT).

As Christians, we yearn to honor God with our speech but often spend more time putting out forest fires created by thoughtless words than dousing smoldering embers. How much better—and more glorifying to God—if we prevent the sparks from erupting in the first place.

Our heavenly Father, the Creator of the universe, humankind, and our mouths, is the source of self-control that can be applied to every aspect of our lives. Even loose lips.

She Meant Well

Michelle Medlock Adams

At that point Peter got up the nerve to ask, "Master, how many times do I forgive a brother or sister who hurts me? Seven?" Jesus replied, "Seven! Hardly. Try seventy times seven."
MATTHEW 18:21–22 MSG

I had been teaching my little heart out at a writers' conference, and I was really tired by day five. As you might imagine, there was little time to eat. So rather than dive into a full-course meal, I opted for a Snickers and a Diet Coke. In fact, I had that same meal a few times throughout the week.

As I headed up the dining hall steps, a woman approached me. She said, "I've been watching you all week. You give so much to others." I smiled, feeling pretty good about myself. She continued, "I've also been watching your eating habits, and I'm worried for you." I thought that was a bizarre statement, but I kept listening. "So," she said, "I have something for you." I smiled, thinking another conferee had a gift for me. Just then, she whipped out a diet plan and said I should prayerfully consider it. Okay, I hadn't seen that one coming.

I wanted to dump my Diet Coke on her head! Some-times, it's really difficult to not become offended. Ask God to help you. And have a Snickers on me!

By the Book

Rachel St. John-Gilbert

A merry heart doeth good like a medicine:
but a broken spirit drieth the bones.
PROVERBS 17:22 KJV

Let's talk about the corporate world, shall we? I know little about it personally, but I've heard quite a bit from my dad. He has thirty years of experience in the aerospace industry with its endless government red tape and rules. People who work in that kind of atmosphere tend to develop survival skills and often manage to really enjoy their jobs.

Now and then in my dad's workplace, some unidentified maverick employee would occasionally write an anonymous piece, spoofing one thing or another in their by-the-book work world. Then the piece would mysteriously appear on someone's desk. That tense recipient, under extreme duress and a deadline, no doubt, would glance at the paper, glance again, drop his pencil, look closely at the paper, and suddenly laugh out loud.

"Hey!" he would call to the person at the next desk, "Look at this!" And off the piece would go on its rounds, brightening everybody's day. Dad brought the following masterpiece home from work when I was in high school, and the whole family gathered round while he read it out loud, pausing now and then to recover from giggles.

Restroom Trip Policy

Effective today a new Restroom Trip Policy (RTP) will be established. Each month, employees will be given twenty Restroom Trip Credits (RTCs). The entrances to all restrooms will be equipped with voice recognition devices. Each employee must provide two copies of voiceprints (one normal, one under stress) to HR. If an employee's credits reach zero, the doors to the restroom will not unlock for that employee's voice until the first of the next month.

In addition, all stalls will be equipped with timed paper roll retractors. If the stall is occupied for more than three minutes, an alarm will sound. Thirty seconds after the alarm sounds, the roll of paper will retract, the toilet will flush, and the door will open.

The RTP is necessary to cut down on dilly-dallying in the restrooms. Thank you in advance for your cooperation.

Clearly someone had had enough "by the bookness" and was, in his own very maverick and funny way, saying, "Lighten up, will ya!"

Dad confirmed to us that yes, rigidity was often a problem in his workplace, but he was also mighty glad to have a good job among people with a great sense of humor.

He gives attention to details, but God has also given him a deep appreciation of his fellow man that makes him a joy to be around. As skilled as Dad is with accuracy and adhering to rules, he would never put those things above showing his care for another person. He also knows how to lighten up. He always left his work at the office, and when he was home, he was ours to enjoy. He's a man who knows how to live by *the* book—the Good Book.

At times it's good to take personal inventory to see if we're really enjoying our lives and bringing joy to those we work with on the job or on a project or at home. Are these areas where you might need to "lighten up a little" with those around you?

May God help us remember that people are always more important than policy and that sometimes a little latitude and understanding will provide just the motivation someone else needs to get a job done—and done well.

Drama Queen

Michelle Medlock Adams

But when the Holy Spirit controls our lives, he will produce this kind of fruit in us: love, joy, peace, patience, kindness, goodness, faithfulness, gentleness, and self-control. Here there is no conflict with the law.
GALATIANS 5:22–23 NLT

I saw a T-shirt the other day that had "Drama Queen" printed on the front of it. I almost bought it because I've been known to be a drama queen from time to time. How about you? Do you have a little theater blood running through your veins, too?

Sure, we all go through our drama queen stages in life, but by the time we enter the workforce, we should have outgrown that phase. However, that's not always the case. Maybe you have a lingering drama queen inside of you, or perhaps you work with a drama queen? If so, you know that "drama queen syndrome" disrupts an office. In fact, it can destroy an otherwise smooth-running workplace. There's no place for drama in the office.

If you wear the drama queen crown from time to time, ask God to help you become more consistent in your Christian walk. Ask Him to help you grow in the fruit of the Spirit. The Bible says that God has crowned you with glory and honor. You don't need that drama queen crown anymore!

Spiritual Life

Cheer Up!

Marilyn Meberg

*The LORD is my strength and my shield; my heart trusts in him,
and I am helped. My heart leaps for joy.*
PSALM 28:7

We were created for perfection. In fact, we were originally placed in a perfect environment. In Eden there were no lingering headaches, digestive challenges, or unsettling sandals. No house would be too large, too small, or too far from the beach. God would supply our desire for the perfect mate as He brought that perfect other to us. God's original design for each of us was to live in a state of perfection. We were created for that experience, and we were created for that expectation.

So what happened? Simply put, Eve disobeyed God and convinced Adam to disobey as well, and the consequence of their disobedience was they were banished from Eden. That meant they lost the perfect environment, the perfect experiences, and the fulfillment of perfect expectations. The reverberating aftermath of their disobedience is our yearning and questing for that which was lost to us. This, then, is why Jesus said, "Here on earth you will have many trials and sorrows" (John 16:33 TLB). It all started with Adam and Eve.

Now, is this so depressing we must dash into the kitchen for a cup of restorative tea? You'll undoubtedly receive momentary comfort from a good (though not perfect) cup of tea. But the loss of perfection need not overwhelm us or depress us. Because Jesus very pragmatically stated we could expect imperfect "stuff" in this world, He prepared us to live a reality-based existence. That knowledge can keep us from being surprised when the trials and sorrows come.

Despite Jesus' warning, often when we experience tribulation we are stunned into a state of self-examination and self-incrimination.

"What did I do wrong?"

"Did I bring this on?"

"Am I being punished?"

"Could this have been avoided?"

"Have I not prayed enough, read scripture enough, witnessed enough, tithed enough?"

The enemy of our souls would love to see us crawl up on that condemnation treadmill and watch us as, with increasing fatigue, we lose our victory and forget that Romans 8:1 states, "There is now no condemnation for those who are in Christ Jesus." We lose sight of the second half of John 16:33, which states, "But be of good cheer, I have overcome the world" (NKJV). That treadmill not only destroys our victory, our sense of value, and our well-being, but it also destroys our faith.

Jesus didn't say, "You've blown it again. Buck up!" Or "Get a grip." When He said, "Cheer up," He gave us cause to be of good cheer and a foundation on which we can rest confidently in the midst of sorrows. Our part is to leap off the treadmill and take God at His Word: "There is now no condemnation." Why? Because I am in Christ Jesus.

Not only can we relax in His provision in the midst of our trials, but hopefully we can also quit the constant, guilt-riddled introspection about our possible responsibility for the pain of life. Then we can focus on being of good cheer and remembering that Christ has overcome all the stuff—big as well as the small—that makes life so imperfect.

Let's repeat: Imperfection, trials, and sorrows all started with disobedience in the Garden. Eve fell for a Satan-devised life, drew her buck-passing husband into it all, and lost paradise. But we can be of good cheer because Christ has overcome the deficits accrued to our account because of Eden.

Now, of course, some trials and sorrows do come to us as a consequence of our poor choices. And some sorrows are ours because we willfully have chosen to yield to the persistent impulse to sin. But that's a different story. . . .

My intent is to remind you that nothing in life is perfect because perfection was lost in Eden. But the flip side of this negative is fully understanding and accepting that life will never be perfect and neither will any experience or relationship. If we can accept that, we can quit looking for it, blaming others or ourselves because we can't find it, and even come to a place of peace about that loss. In fact, we might even cheer up a bit as we quit the search. . .the pressure to find perfection is over. That gives me the energy to settle down to a platter of pasta that is a trifle overdone with a touch too little garlic—and not lose my joy.

Lone Laughers

Rachel St. John-Gilbert

Eye hath not seen, nor ear heard, neither have entered into the heart
of man, the things which God hath prepared for them that love him.
1 CORINTHIANS 2:9 KJV

Growing up attending a nondenominational Bible church, I remember logging many hours listening to skilled pastors and seminarians expound upon beloved passages of scripture. But even the most eloquent of expositors would occasionally get tongue-tied.

My family valued humor *almost* as much as faith, so when the preacher made a slip of the lip, one of us often hid behind his or her hymnal, trying desperately to gain control. Often the poor soul was the *only* one in the audience whose funny bone had been so dangerously activated. I was not immune.

One Sunday evening when I was a teen, I listened to an esteemed graduate of Dallas Theological Seminary preach on Moses and his encounter with God in the burning bush. With all the drama Dr. Jones could muster, he held his Bible aloft.

"Moses!" he cried in his rich, beautiful voice, "Take off your feet! You're standing on holy ground!"

I began to giggle, quietly at first, hoping I could stifle myself. My girlfriend, Lou Ann, was sitting beside me, and her shoulders began to quake.

So now I had company, but it only made my situation worse as I couldn't resist embellishing the blooper further. I regained control of myself long enough to whisper to my friend, "Bet he had a hard time getting down that mountain without his feet on."

My buddy and I snorted and expected one of our parents to appear and march us out of the sanctuary by our ears.

My parents, however, have had their own brushes with disgrace. On their first visit to a new Sunday school class, they heard the teacher announce that a group from Jungle Aviation and Radio Service would visit the church. The church needed volunteers to provide a meal. The teacher finished his appeal by saying, "We really need some volunteers to cook and serve those people in JARS."

My parents immediately sank behind their Bibles, struggling for control.

Another time my sister endured what must have been the most uncomfortable prayer service of her life. She heard a young man with the most nasal tone of voice she'd ever heard lay out a string of requests addressed to the Almighty with an incredible number of "eths" added.

"Dear Father," he intoned. "Blesseth Thoueth thiseth meeting here-eth in Thy presence." Giggles bubbled up inside Becky like a newly opened bottle of ginger ale, threatening to burst from her mouth and nose. She instinctively cupped her mouth with one hand and her nose with the other. This action resulted in an emission that sounded like a suckling pig. Then there was a blessed pause. *Whew, perhaps I'm saved!* she thought. But no. He began again, "And ifeth it pleaseth Thou. . ."

At this point my poor sister began to wheeze. It was the prayereth that hadeth no endeth.

Most of us who have attended church over a lifetime have a story to tell about bloopers spotted in a church bulletin. Someone passed the following jewels to me via cyberspace:

- This morning's sermon is entitled "Jesus Walks on Water." This evening's sermon is entitled, "Searching for Jesus."
- Please place your donation in the envelope along with the deceased person you want remembered.
- This evening at 7:00 p.m. come join in our 10th Annual Hymn Sing. Come prepared to sin!
- The Associate Minister unveiled our new tithing campaign slogan last Sunday: "I Upped MY Pledge. Up YOURS!"

The scriptures indicate that a merry heart is good medicine. With all the stress in the world, perhaps that's one reason God doesn't let the faithful take themselves too seriously for too long! Meanwhile, keep those tissues ready to fake a good cry or sneeze if you land in the unenviable position of being the Lone Laugher.

Hidden or Not?

Karon Phillips Goodman

If we live in the Spirit, let us also walk in the Spirit.
GALATIANS 5:25 NKJV

Do you look at day planners with their five thousand lines per page and get bleary-eyed? I do, despite the control and peace they promise. It's as if I should be able to fill every line with something profound and then, heaven forbid, should I forget any of it. The trusty notebook thicker than my dictionary may promise to streamline and organize my life, but mostly it just intimidates me. And I'm afraid to get within a hundred miles of one of those electronic calendars. With my computer (dis)abilities, I'd black out the West Coast.

Logistics and technology aren't second nature to me, but like all good, overly involved, micromanaging, obsessive maniacs, I'd fallen prey for years to the "urgency of the details" of my life. I didn't get control or peace, though. I got migraines and a sick stomach. I was possessed by the cultural mission: Achieve! Conquer! Excel! (and never be late, behind, or off course). It wasn't a life—it was a perpetual final exam in quantum physics: "Your mission, should you choose to accept, is to do everything in the world, be everything to the world, all at once, all by yourself. Describe the steps, and neatness counts."

Gladly. Step 1: Drive myself crazy. Step 2: Repeat Step 1.

Clearly, I would have flunked the test. But guess what? The Master Teacher intervened and let me start with Him.

"What are you looking for?" He asked me.

"Peace," I whimpered, tired and bent from the search.

"Would a simpler life bring you peace? Do you want a little more order to your world? Is insight for all your decisions what you need?"

How'd He get so smart?

"Yep, that would do it. Know where I can find all that?"

He laughed. "It'll find you."

Now, that was helpful. You mean, it isn't within the pages of my calendar, not deduced from a calculus-like logic? I've been going about this all wrong?

"And how, pray tell, in my complicated life will it all find me?" I asked.

"It's already here, and having it is your choice. The world will always be complicated, but your life doesn't have to be. It all depends on what possesses you. Would you like Me to explain?"

Now it was my turn to laugh. "Uh, yes, I'm going to need the whole recipe here. Let me kick some of this clutter out of the way, and we'll get started, if You dare."

He came closer. "Not to worry. The peace you want— My peace—is already living inside you. Let Me wrap you in it and tell you everything."

God Gives You Wisdom

Ramona Richards

*If any of you need wisdom, you should ask God, and it will be
given to you. God is generous and won't correct you for asking.*
JAMES 1:5 CEV

The older I've gotten, the more I've heard myself uttering the words, "Well, as my mother used to say. . ." It's almost become a joke among my friends, and they'll start to grin even before I can get some pithy proverb out. In fact, some of my mother's sayings are quite humorous, filled with homespun advice and earthy metaphors, like the day she was canning some beans and told me she was "hotter than a tent preacher in July." We're from Alabama, and I can assure you that camp meetings in the summer can get pretty hot!

It's not just the down-to-earth proverbs, however, that I depend on. My mother's wisdom sometimes amazes me. I began to ask her advice on people and situations when I was still just a kid, and she has seldom steered me wrong. When a kid was trying to bully me in junior high school, her advice helped me ease the situation in just a few days. When dealing with a variety of men in college had me spinning in confusion, she helped me find my feet again. She taught me how to handle money, work, even my faith.

I once asked her about the source of her wisdom, and she responded, "A little bit of living and a whole lot of prayer."

My mother had learned to rely on God for guidance and inspiration, which had made her invaluable to her friends and family. Even the tiniest problems were turned over to God, which gave her the confidence to help out those who came to her for advice.

I think it's very revealing that wisdom in scripture is portrayed as a woman (see Proverbs 1:20–21), since women seem to have an instinctual sense of how to take the little lessons of life and scripture and use them to nurture those they love. Even more encouraging is this reminder from James, that if we ever feel we're lacking in wisdom, all we have to do is ask—and God will provide both wisdom and the confidence to use it.

Less or More?

Karon Phillips Goodman

*"These things I have spoken to you, that in Me you may have peace.
In the world you will have tribulation; but be of good cheer,
I have overcome the world."*
JOHN 16:33 NKJV

I thought about this passage one day. *Sure, the world, but have You seen my calendar, my closet? Want to take a peek at my checkbook?* I challenged silently.

Know what He said?

"I am all the peace you will ever need, and I live to breathe it on you now and forever. Don't worry about all that stuff you can see. Let's start with what you can't."

Well, that sounded anything but simple. Thought I'd better clarify.

"You mean the anxiety and worry and doubt and stress and clutter in my heart? The complications I put there myself, right?"

"Yes, and that's far worse than the schedule and bills and dishes and laundry and everything else you're complaining about."

"Hey! I have a lot to do!" I protested.

He smiled, and His eyes twinkled like those of a toddler

with a secret. "I know. And there's even more to come. I can't wait to be a part of it."

Something makes me think I'm going to want to start a new to-do list.

Peace in abundance. . . Before we address the clutter and chaos—that we can touch and that we can't—we need something more. Our lives aren't complicated because they're full. They're complicated because they're full of the wrong things. More of the God we need means less of everything we don't. It's so simple even I can understand.

Call it physics, call it faith, call it whatever you want. But your heart—and your home—will hold only so much. You decide what each is filled with. More of God's peace in my heart means less of my emptiness for it. More space in my home means less stuff in my way. The tangible and the intangible both adapt to the laws of science. And I can make my life and my home less complicated when I recognize how everything hinges on that choice: more of one thing, less of another. The Lord says I can start making that choice right now.

So before you prioritize your committee memberships, color code your wardrobe, or make a trip to the city dump with the stuff from your living room floor, would you like to join me on this quest for more in our lives—more of the peace and strength and wisdom of God? It's your choice. The complicated world around you will always be there, and you can possess it if you want. Or you can be possessed by the love and power and grace of God. You can have more of God beginning today, ending never, if you choose. And you don't have to be any smarter or braver than you are right now. God is quite the rescuer.

WORDS A WOMAN WILL NEVER SAY

"Hmm, let's see. I have so much to wear, it's too easy for me to choose."

Pump It Up

Michelle Medlock Adams

*Through Him, therefore, let us constantly and at all times offer up
to God a sacrifice of praise, which is the fruit of lips that thankfully
acknowledge and confess and glorify His name.*
HEBREWS 13:15 AMP

Be honest. . .you were feeling pretty content in your job
and your overall life until you ran into her. She drove up
in her new Cadillac Escalade, pulled in next to you, and shared
how she'd just been hired to a new position that pays three
times what you currently make. And to top it off, she just lost
fourteen pounds on the South Beach Diet. Suddenly, all of
your contentment vanished. Instead, that contentment was
replaced with resentment, jealousy, and a little bit of anger.

If you've ever experienced a situation similar to this one,
you know how miserable it can make you. It can totally rob
your joy. There's only one way to fight off the resentment
and jealousy that follow an encounter like the one described
above. You have to pump up the praise. That's right—praise
the Lord like you've never praised before. Don't dwell on
what you don't have. Meditate on what you do have. Praise
God for the good things in your life. And praise Him for the
blessings in your friend's life, too. Praise will bring peace and
contentment to your heart, and it's a lot more fun than the
South Beach Diet.

Know the Truth, Tell the Truth

Karon Phillips Goodman

Teach me your way, O LORD, and I will walk in your truth;
give me an undivided heart, that I may fear your name.
PSALM 86:11

If you and I ever meet, you might want to bring along an interpreter. I've traveled little in my life and perhaps have become a bit too comfortable with my Southern drawl. I know Miss Ruby at my local print shop understands that "ma'am" is a three-syllable word for me, but I didn't realize how likely others would be to have trouble.

My husband and I visited the Grand Canyon not long ago. Of course, it's spectacular and worth the "saddle sores" of thirty-five hundred miles, and everyone there and along the way was wonderful. But sooner or later, I'd have to open my mouth. Then they'd look at me with eyes that said, "I know she looks like she's from this planet, but what is that language she's speaking?" They'd stop all activity, focusing their stares on my face like someone trying to understand a doctor explaining a rare medical condition. I'd repeat myself and use visual aids, like point to a map or a picture on a menu, and try to slow my speech even more. After the third or so try, they'd catch enough words to get the idea, answer quickly, and draw one of those "Wow, unbelievable!" breaths. Still, they were nice.

I think sometimes God feels like I did on my trip. He knows He's using words we should understand. He's fairly sure we're awake, He's made things as simple as possible, and yet we stand there going, "Huh?" Our misunderstanding, though, is more one of disbelief than language patterns. Can He really be telling me the truth when He says He'll be with me always? Can my life with Him really have the peace and simplicity He promises?

We hear His words, but we complicate the message. Sometimes we're almost a little suspicious of His absolute love. Maybe He's speaking another planet's language, and "I forgive you" really means "Gotcha!" Maybe "You are Mine" is really code for "Mess up again, and I'm done with you." But no, His love is simple and at the birth of all peace. Unlike an accent we squint our ears to understand, God's Word is simple and clear and unchanging, because His attitude matches His actions. And we can follow His example.

Knowledge Is Power

Michelle Medlock Adams

My people are ruined because they don't know what's right or true.
HOSEA 4:6 MSG

Q: What do you call it when a blond dyes her hair brunette?

A: Artificial intelligence.

Entire Web sites are dedicated to dumb-blond jokes. Even though I'm not a natural blond (There, I said it!), I take blond jokes quite personally. No one wants to be thought of as an airhead or a clueless person. That's definitely not attractive. While it's fun to watch dumb blonds in movies and television sitcoms, in real life being dumb (whether you're blond, redheaded, or brunette) is not a laughing matter.

Oh, sure, we all have our clueless moments from time to time. When you get older, they call them "senior moments." I guess before you qualify for senior discounts, they are called "blond moments." Whatever you want to call them, they happen. Most of the time they are harmless—like locking your keys in the car or momentarily forgetting the name of a friend or associate. These are simple lapses in memory—not a lack of knowledge. There's a difference.

The Old Testament prophet Hosea wrote that God's

people were being destroyed by a lack of knowledge. In other words, what you don't know *will* hurt you. That's why we need to know God's Word. We need to understand our promises and covenant rights and walk in them every single day. God created us and then left us an owner's manual—the Bible. It's a road map for life. In it you'll discover the paths that lead to health, wholeness, peace, renewed strength, and a beautiful life. But if we don't take time to read it and memorize it and meditate on its words, then we will lack knowledge. Maybe that lack of knowledge won't cause physical death, but it might cause the death of a relationship or the loss of a job.

The world has taken this biblical principle and created the slogan "Knowledge is power." Maybe you've heard it before. Well, that's really true. When you have knowledge of God's Word, you will be empowered. Even your "blond moments" will be fewer and farther between. Wisdom is a beautiful thing, and there is wisdom in the Word—so get it!

Technology

Toni Sortor

*"Oh, for the days when I was in my prime, when. . .
my children were around me."*
JOB 29:4–5

I venture into new technologies kicking and screaming. I learn what I need to learn, but I never enjoy it. To this day, I cannot program a new number into my telephone's quick-dial system, and I break into a sweat when I have to change a toner cartridge.

Downloading e-mail attachments gives me great concern. What if I push the wrong button and send an important file off into the universe, never to be seen again?

Fortunately my husband and grown sons are geeks (I say this with profound respect). They zip around my computer, installing new programs and updates whenever needed. My only complaint is when one of them changes the settings on my desk chair and I find my feet no longer touch the floor.

One day I told my eldest son I had fallen in love with the first computer game I ever paid for only to find he had been playing the same game for months. We exchanged hints, and while he did most of the instructing, I had found a few tricks to give to him. I swear I saw a little glimmer of respect in his eyes that day. I was still a computer baby, but maybe there was hope for me, after all. I'll never love technology, but it has brought some good things into my life, including something in common with my adult sons, which I consider a blessing.

Is the Proverbs 31 Woman for Real?

Dena Dyer

Charm is deceptive, and beauty is fleeting;
but a woman who fears the LORD is to be praised.
PROVERBS 31:30

Do you ever feel intimidated by the Proverbs 31 woman—the one who sewed like Betsy Ross, volunteered like Mother Teresa, and ran her own business like Oprah? I know I have.

But I have a theory about that "perfect" biblical woman. As we know, Solomon wrote Proverbs, and Solomon had hundreds of wives. So, dear reader, I believe the Proverbs 31 woman was a composite. Solomon simply took the best qualities from several wives and created a word portrait of his "ideal" companion. (It works for me!)

Seriously, I've often felt discouraged while reading that famous biblical chapter. I can't tell the difference between soufflé and flambé, and—to my mother's horror—I can't even sew on a button. I've ruined laundry, sent "belated birthday" cards, and taken my kid to preschool in my pajamas more times than I can count.

For years, every time I read Proverbs 31, I felt as if this spiritual superwoman was up in heaven, mocking my paltry attempts at being a wife, friend, mom, and daughter. I didn't realize that the chapter was most likely an overview of the woman's entire life (and not one day, week, or even month)— or that, as my friend and fellow author Char Barnes says, "In Proverbs 31, the woman's children rise up and call her blessed. Toddlers don't rise up and bless their mother—this lady obviously had grown children."

After I began to experience panic attacks because of my perfectionism, I realized God was calling me to a different standard than the one I had erroneously set for myself. And through the wisdom of a godly counselor, I discovered that in the verse I had taken as my mantra—"Be perfect, therefore, as your heavenly Father is perfect" (Matthew 5:48)—the word "perfect" can also be translated as "mature."

Part of my becoming mature has meant learning that I have limits. We have just one life, and our Savior died and rose again so that it could be an abundant life. When Jesus said in John 10:10, "I have come that they may have life, and have it to the full," He wasn't talking about a day planner jam-packed with activities or a schedule crammed with "to-dos."

Christ was speaking about a life of purpose, contentment, and peace. As a busy wife and mom, I've come to believe that we can experience abundant life daily if we get off the hamster wheel of perfectionism, recognize our limits, and nestle close to Jesus.

When I remember that He loved me enough to leave the perfection of heaven and soil His feet with the crud of earth,

I can see myself as He does. I can accept God's mercy and impart that mercy to the imperfect people around me.

Then—and only then—can I live each day with joy and *perfect* peace.

Embarrassing Moments

Tina Krause

"There is nothing concealed that will not be disclosed, or hidden that will not be made known. What you have said in the dark will be heard in the daylight, and what you have whispered in the ear in the inner rooms will be proclaimed from the roofs." (And what I buy at the pharmacy will be announced by an automated voice.)
LUKE 12:2–3

Embarrassing moments follow me like baby ducks trailing their mother. Like the time I was running late so I slipped a jacket over my nightgown to drive my sons to school. Racing home to get dressed for work, a police officer flagged me down. Making hand motions, I indicated I was unable to step out of the car for fear of violating public exposure laws. As the law enforcer approached my car, I clutched my jacket around me and slithered down into the seat, remaining outwardly calm, albeit undignified. With a smile and a nod, I pretended my "nightie" was a new line of casual wear, praying he wouldn't notice but certain that he did.

So today I had another one of those moments. I was scheduled to have X-rays taken, but—due to hormonal irregularities—I feared the unthinkable. Before proceeding with the X-rays, I decided to take one of those "home tests" just to be safe.

Buying one of those kits at my age is worse than dragging toilet tissue from one's shoe while walking down the center aisle of church. When I finally mustered the courage to go to the pharmacy, my goal was to buy the kit with as little fanfare as possible.

Aiming for discretion, I bought other items with the test, even though I didn't need them, hoping the kit would slip by the clerk unnoticed. As she scanned the items, I initiated conversation to draw attention away from the box. It worked. The visions I had of her looking at me and then eyeing the box with a curious grin failed to materialize.

I thought I was home free as I exited the store, but as the automatic door swung open an alarm resounded, complete with an automated voice instructing me to return to the checkout counter. With all eyes on me, I scurried back as the salesclerk announced loud enough for the entire line of waiting people to hear, "Oh, I'm sorry. It must be your home pregnancy test!"

The humiliation of living somewhere between kneesocks and support hose served as another reminder that the secrets I try hardest to conceal are the ones most often exposed.

Actually, my attempts to disguise the real me fail more often than a student who refuses to attend class. But I've found a solution: Face the embarrassment and go on. And (ahem) pray I never run into that salesclerk or police officer again.

"Don't Hate Me because I'm Beautiful"

Michelle Medlock Adams

Yet you are stupid enough to brag, and it is wrong to be so proud.
JAMES 4:16 CEV

You've seen the commercial. The gorgeous girl whips her long, luscious locks to the side, then with her pouty, very glossy lips, she utters, "Don't hate me because I'm beautiful."

But in reality, we would hate her—not because she's beautiful. No, we'd hate her because she loves to brag on herself. Let's face it; nobody likes a bragger. (You're thinking of someone right now, aren't you?) We all know someone like that girl in the commercial. She might not be as blatant, but you can bet your lipstick she'll find a way to sneak in a boast or two.

She might not even brag about herself. She might brag about her new home. Or worse, she might drone on and on about her superaccomplished kids. (Her car bumpers are covered with MY KID IS AN HONOR STUDENT stickers. Okay, I have those bumper stickers, too. Sorry.) No matter what she brags about, it's enough to make you want to run for the hills. Am I right?

Let me ask you another question. Are you a bragger?

Do you love talking on and on about yourself? It's an easy habit to fall into, but it's also a very dangerous one. The Bible says that pride comes before a fall, and that fall may plop you right into a pit of loneliness. Friends will start avoiding you. Family members will dread your annual brag letter, er um, Christmas letter. People will hate you—but it won't be because you're beautiful. So don't go there!

If you're struggling with the bad habit of bragging, ask God to put a watch over your mouth. Make a conscious decision to listen more than you talk. And more than anything, learn to trust God to raise you up. You'll discover that you won't have to brag on yourself to feel important. God has a big ol' brag book, and He will find ways to lift you up and give you favor with those around you. You'll win friends and influence people, and they'll love you because you're beautiful on the inside. After all, that's where it really counts!

Supermarket Loyalty: Looking Out for Number One

Rachel St. John-Gilbert

" 'Love the Lord your God with all your heart and with all your soul and with all your mind.' This is the first and greatest commandment."
MATTHEW 22:37–38

So what do you think about the new "Preferred Customer" card at your local supermarket? The first one at the first store kinda makes you feel among the elite, right? Card-carrying shoppers are treated to two-for-one rutabagas and a free bottle of children's vitamins with every purchase of Sugar Poofs cereal—the antidote right along with the poison. Such a deal, dahling! One locally owned store in our small town has upped the ante in the War for Regulars with the guilt-inducing tactic of designating their cards "Loyalty Cards."

Well, I wanted to be loyal, but I soon found every other supermarket in town was also giving out preferred customer cards—and I took them all. In my fleeting moments of rock-solid self-assertion, it doesn't bother me that my Brookstone Loyalty Card lies within my purse, nestled in a stack of a dozen or so preferred customer cards. Yet, in my weaker moments of irrational empathy, I feel I am a Grocery Adulteress. How can I live with myself when I shun the down-home smiles and "Can I hep ya" service of this locally owned store—when I run wantonly into the arms of every grocery store within a ten-mile radius of my house looking for great deals?

The last time I bought groceries at Brookstone's, I squirmed while I checked out. I recognized the handsome, clean-cut checker. Ever chipper and polite, Cody was dressed in a crisp white shirt and black skinny tie and greeted me with a beaming smile.

"Good morning, Mrs. St. John! Do you have your loyalty card today?"

"Why, yes, I do!" I smiled nervously. I began pawing through my billfold for the card from Cody's store. I couldn't put my fingers right on it, so I tried to act nonchalant while blindly searching through my purse. At the same time, I conversed with Nice Tie Guy. After pulling out a gas card, credit card, and a movie rental card, I dumped the contents of my purse on the conveyor belt. Picking through my multicolored stack of preferred customer cards, sweating profusely from the shame, I searched wildly for the black one with "Brookstone's" written in red letters. I finally found it.

"See?" I smiled weakly and handed over the prized piece of plastic. "I told you I had it."

Cody looked pained, while I gathered my lipstick, pens, and a couple of pink pouches of feminine pads from the conveyor belt. He said not a word. He didn't have to. I felt so cheap.

Loyalty can be hard to give, especially when we make decisions based upon self-interest—when we don't consider the impact on our relationships with others and with God. If our loyalty is divided between the enticing "deals" this world offers vs. what God offers, we may squirm when He asks to see our Spiritual Loyalty Card.

May our desire to honor Him outweigh the pull of the world. And may the Grocery Bag of Our Lives be filled with words and deeds that reflect a heart loyal to Him.

Malls

Toni Sortor

But godliness with contentment is great gain. For we brought nothing into the world, and we can take nothing out of it.
1 TIMOTHY 6:6–7

Our area has first-class shopping malls every two or three miles on the highway, complete with restaurants, rides for the kids, bowling lanes, theaters, and ice rinks. I hate them all. You can't buy any clothing larger than a size four there. I can spend hours wandering a mall here and never find what I need. It's easier to go downtown and not find what I need.

Yet when we're on vacation I love malls. They fill up a rainy day and give some indication of the spirit of the area, what the people there care about and need in their lives. I especially love malls without a single "designer" store but two or three outdoor supply stores carrying rough woolen jackets, rain gear that keeps you 100 percent dry, and locally made leather shoes.

These malls are small and friendly. They smell of good leather and wet wool, not some French fragrance. The bookstores are full of good mysteries and local lore; the bestseller lists are not displayed by the cash register. The clerks go out of their way to be helpful; the shoppers smile a lot. They are what downtowns used to be before the malls went up on the edges of America. But I bet the residents of that vacation area hate their own malls and can't wait to visit mine. The cement is always grayer on the other side of the fence, you see.

WORDS A WOMAN WILL NEVER SAY
"What do you say we cut short our shopping spree and check out that auto show at the race car arena?"

Lipstick and Oil Slicks

Rachel St. John-Gilbert

*But when you are tempted, he will also provide
a way out so that you can stand up under it.*
1 CORINTHIANS 10:13

On the day I began to write this book in earnest, the sun was shining and the air was crisp. Laptop in hand, I headed to one of my favorite bistros near a peaceful park. Yep, this was the writing life—having a bona fide excuse to be liberated from laundry, dishes, and children. Able to act artsy, free-spirited, and fancy-free. . .to write about life's little pleasures or important social issues like the spiritual implications of earthy humor.

After savoring each bite of my roasted chicken pesto sandwich and every sip of my black currant tea, I beelined to the ladies' room to wash my hands before attacking my laptop with inspired fervor. As I reached into my purse to grab my lipstick, I felt my makeup bag sticking to my hand.

"Oh no!" I moaned as I looked at a thin layer of a sticky black substance covering my entire palm. "*Great!* I must have a leaky pen."

Determined not to let this ruin my Bohemian mood, I simply soaped up a second time. Carefully reopening my purse to locate that pesky pen, I detected a pungent odor. Rummaging deeper into the bottomless cavern of my handbag, to my horror, I realized that I had somehow left the top off a bottle of natural sweetener. The dark syrupy liquid had doused my belongings, with nary an escapee.

As I surveyed the scope of my situation, I laid out a roll of paper towels and began to fish out the contents of my purse. It looked like the Exxon Valdez oil spill, and I was on a rescue mission.

The irony of my plight was as thick as the goop covering my stuff: I had used this sweetener for its greater health benefits, and instead, now I was experiencing so much stress that it would take a hot-stone massage, a detox footbath, and a week of coffee enemas to undo the damage—not to mention the damper it put on my writing mood.

Here I was, all set to write inspirational humor in the vein of Steinbeck (oops, *Bombeck*) and now I was complaining under my breath in the ladies' restroom, wondering how on earth I could salvage my things.

Twenty minutes and a roll of paper towels later, I had the situation under control. Although I smelled like prune juice, I thanked God I caught the leak before it had oozed out of my purse and onto my laptop.

Isn't that the way life is sometimes? A little leak left untended can wreak a lot of destruction. Take sin for instance. Satan tempts us with something sweet—maybe even something good for us like an inheritance or a job or a ministry. Then he leaves the bottle cap slightly askew. Before you know it, if we allow it, that something sweet becomes a sticky mess, and we're stuck in an oil spill of backsliding. We let our inheritance fuel our greed instead of our generosity; we spend more time on the job than with our kids; our ministry becomes all consuming and we lose our joy.

But God is on a rescue mission, and He offers a way of escape. He's good at capping sin if we'll let Him. When *He* cleans up our messes, He leaves no telltale residue behind.

Follow the Directions—Exactly!

Michelle Medlock Adams

*Now if you will faithfully obey me, you will be my very own people.
The whole world is mine.*
EXODUS 19:5 CEV

Recently, talk show queen Oprah Winfrey revealed that she lives in shaper panties. She shared that clothes just look better over them, pointing out that spandex shaper undergarments hold everything in its place without any visible panty lines. *Well,* I thought, *that sounds good to me.* I went on a quest to buy the specific brand of shaper undies that Oprah mentioned on her show, but apparently every other woman in America did the same thing. They were sold out! So I settled for a different brand that promised to deliver the exact same results.

They are probably all the same, I figured, *so I'll just make do with this off-brand.*

Big mistake!

The shaper panties I bought had some weird spandex around the upper thigh that made the leg part of the panties bulge out. That's a nice look—bulging fat spilling forth beneath spandex leg bands. It was disastrous. And what's worse, I couldn't return them because they were underwear!

So now I dust the house with my shaper panties. (At least I found something they are good for!) My problem? I didn't follow Oprah's exact directions. I didn't buy the shaper undies she recommended. I bought an off-brand, and the results were *so* not good.

You know, it's the same way with God. If you don't follow His exact directions, the results are never as good as they could have been, and sometimes they're disastrous. If you know in your heart that God has told you to volunteer for the Sunday school superintendent position at your church but you'd rather be in charge of the Christmas musical because there's a lot more glory associated with it—watch out. I see bad spiritual panty lines in your future!

If you go ahead and disregard the Holy Spirit's leading and take on the Christmas musical, it will probably be one of the hardest tasks you've ever done. See, God doesn't want our sacrifice; He wants our obedience.

Walking in obedience to God is much more than just obeying the Ten Commandments. It's about listening to His leading and following His exact directions. If you miss God once in a while but your heart is right, don't worry. God will find you. But make a decision today to walk in obedience. If you do, you'll be in good shape—no matter what you wear!

The Ice Cream Man Cometh: Fear, Faith, and a Changing World

Rachel St. John-Gilbert

"Do not let your hearts be troubled. Trust in God; trust also in me."
JOHN 14:1

I cherish the childhood memory of the sweet music ringing out from an ice cream truck. At the first faint note of "Three Blind Mice," my heart began to race, and I ran through the house frantically looking for Mom and a shiny dime. We lived on a court, and I can still remember the flood of relief I felt when I found the ice cream truck at a standstill, with the ice cream man filling orders for half a dozen neighbor kids. My treasure secured, I would sit with my buddies on the curb in front of my house, peeling the chocolate coating off our Eskimo Pies, letting it melt slowly on our tongues.

Well, those wonder years are far behind me now, and past Popsicles seem to have melted into a permanent part of my behind. Consequently, I do penance for pleasures past and present by jogging each afternoon in my neighborhood around 4 p.m. Recently, I heard the faint music of "The Entertainer" and was pleased to see that the ice cream truck still cometh. Upon first sighting the big white truck, I took a pleasant momentary trip down memory lane. But on subsequent outings, I've digressed into a suspicious frame of mind.

A lot of construction is going on in our neighborhood, and many vacant lots are sprinkled among the completed homes. For some reason, the ice cream man seems to crisscross my running route, and I start feeling eerily vulnerable as I hear the truck approaching the street I'm on. To make matters worse, from a distance, the driver looks like Popeye's nemesis, Brutus—a big, burly kind of a guy.

In my moments of insecurity, I think, *Hmm. I wonder if that guy is really selling ice cream or if he's cruising for unsuspecting, slightly overweight women who can't run very fast.* Cleverly, I wave to an imaginary neighbor in the distance and holler, "Hi, Bob!" so it appears I'm being noticed and would be sorely missed if I suddenly disappeared.

Then I mentally rehearse a personal safety plan so that if—God forbid—the ice cream man tried to drag me into his truck, I would be ready. First, I would grab two fudge pops and shove them into his eyes. While he was flinging frozen globs of chocolate mush from his perverted peepers, I'd grab the microphone to the truck's sound system and yell, "Free ice cream! Hurry!" In a matter of seconds, mommies and kiddies would run out of nowhere like the Amish answering a clanging bell for help from a neighboring farm—and I would be rescued. After the cops dragged the ice cream criminal away, I would dole out free frozen treats from the back of the truck. I would receive a badge of courage from the mayor while the news cameras rolled and strains from the Rocky theme song blared over the truck's speakers.

And then, feeling a little sheepish, I wonder: Maybe the

ice cream man is a nice guy who is working a second job to make ends meet for his family. Maybe he's a big, burly man because, well, he likes ice cream. And maybe he crisscrosses my running route because it happens to be his route.

And yet, times have, indeed, changed since I was a kid. We do have to focus more on personal safety. But does this relegate us to live a life of fear? Maybe our goal as believers should be to strike a balance between reasonable readiness and unflinching faith that God is our Protector.

So the next time you're tempted to dwell on a worst-case scenario, give it to God in prayer. Then look for the nearest place to chill out with your favorite ice cream cone.

Experiencing Happily Ever After

Michelle Medlock Adams

*So put on all the armor that God gives. Then when that
evil day comes, you will be able to defend yourself.
And when the battle is over, you will still be standing firm.*
EPHESIANS 6:13 CEV

I love fairy tales. My daughters love fairy tales, too. Even the offbeat ones like *Shrek*. Have you ever noticed that in a fairy tale there's usually a damsel in distress? Typically, there is a beautiful princess who is held captive in a tower that is surrounded by a moat full of alligators and the occasional fire-breathing dragon. She waits in that tower, hoping that someday her prince will come. She dreams about the day a valiant knight on his white horse will ride up to the castle, slay the dragon, use the alligators as stepping-stones, climb up the tower, and rescue her.

Maybe you've had that dream yourself. Well, stop dreaming, sister! Your dream has already come true, and it's heavenly! Your Prince (the Prince of Peace) has already come on His white horse. He rescued you from that tower of sin more than two thousand years ago. And He didn't just rescue you. He also took away your victim status and made you into a victor! He turned you into an overcomer. He even gave you armor—the full armor of God—to protect you as you fight evil and rescue others from that fire-breathing dragon—aka Satan.

Sure, fairy tales are fun to watch on the big screen, but I don't want to be a damsel in distress in real life. A princess—yes. A damsel in distress—no. God doesn't want you to be a damsel in distress, either. If you've been living with a victim's mentality for too long, it's time to wise up to the Word. God says that you are more than a conqueror through Christ Jesus. His Word says that you are highly favored. It says that God did not give you a spirit of fear. The Word says that we can use God's mighty weapons to knock down the devil's strongholds. Like evangelist Jesse Duplantis always says, "I read the back of the Book, and we win!"

Your damsel-in-distress days are behind you. You are a winner. You are a beautiful princess—a member of God's royal family. In *Beauty and the Beast*, you get to be Beauty. In *Cinderella*, you get to be the lovely Cinderella. In *Shrek*, you get to be. . .er, uh, Princess Fiona (when she isn't an ogre). And if you've made Jesus the Lord of your life, you are promised an eternity of "happily ever after." Now that's a story worth sharing!

Acknowledgments

Barbour Publishing, Inc. expresses its appreciation to all those who generously gave permission to reprint and/or adapt any copyrighted material. Diligent effort has been made to identify, locate, and contact copyright holders, and to secure permission to use copyrighted material. If any permissions or acknowledgments have been inadvertently omitted, or if such permissions were not received by the time of publication, the publisher would sincerely appreciate receiving complete information so that correct credit can be given in future editions.

"Laughter and Hairpins," "She Meant Well," "Drama Queen," "Walk in Love," and "Pump It Up" by Michelle Medlock Adams, from *Daily Wisdom for Working Women* © 2004. Published by Barbour Publishing, Inc., Uhrichsville, OH. Used by permission.

"Makeup—Don't Leave Home without It," "Bring on the Legwarmers," "Blind Faith," "God Loves You—Flaws and All," "Don't Hate Me because I'm Beautiful," "Step into the Light," "Bulldog Faith," "Follow the Directions—Exactly!" "Don't Be Moved!" "Expert Opinions—No Thanks!" "Be the Glue," "Experiencing Happily Ever After," and "Knowledge Is Power" by Michelle Medlock Adams, from *Secrets of Beauty* © 2005. Published by Barbour Publishing, Inc., Uhrichsville, OH. Used by permission.

"Brain Workouts" and "Rx: Chocolate" by Martha Bolton, from *I Think, Therefore I Have a Headache!* © 2003. Used by permission of Bethany House, a division of Baker Publishing Group, Grand Rapids, MI.

About Our Contributors

Michelle Medlock Adams has a diverse résumé featuring inspirational books, children's picture books, magazine articles, web copy and greeting cards. Author of thirty-eight books, her insights have appeared in "Today's Christian Woman," "Brio," and "American Cheerleader." She is also an inspirational speaker. She lives in Bedford, Indiana, with her husband, Jeff. They have two teenage daughters, Abby and Allyson. Visit www.michellemedlockadams.com.

Martha Bolton is a full-time comedy writer and the author of more than fifty books. She was a staff writer for Bob Hope for fifteen years and wrote for Phyllis Diller, Ann Jillian, and many others. She has received four Angel Awards, an Emmy nomination, and a Dove award nomination.

Patsy Clairmont is a speaker with the Women of Faith conferences and bestselling author of titles like *God Uses Cracked Pots*, and *Normal Is Just a Setting on Your Dryer*. Patsy has been married to Les for more than forty years. They have two sons, Marty and Jason; daughter-in-law Danya; and grandsons, Justin and Noah.

Deb Coty, a resident of Seffner, Florida, is an events speaker, columnist, and author of *The Distant Shore*, and *Hugs, Humor, and Hope for Harried Moms*. She is coauthor of *Grit for the Oyster: 250 Pearls of Wisdom for Aspiring Writers*, and a contributor to Barbour's 365 Daily Whispers of Wisdom for. . . series, including Busy Women, Wives, and Girls.

Dena Dyer is a wife, mom, and speaker/entertainer from Texas. She enjoys reminding women that Jesus is our stability in a chaotic world, and she dreams about writing the next "Great American Novel." She and her husband, Carey, are raising two boys with fear and trembling—and *lots* of prayer!

Author and speaker **Karon Phillips Goodman** lives in Alabama and loves to talk with other women about God's grace and our total and splendid dependency on Him. Karon's latest title is *Pursued by the Shepherd: Every Woman's Journey from Lost to Found*. Contact Karon at karongoodman.com.

Tina Krause is an award-winning newspaper columnist, freelance writer, and author of *Laughter Therapy* (Barbour Publishing, 2002). Her articles have appeared in forty-five magazines and fourteen book compilations. Tina is a mom to two sons and "Nana" to four grandchildren. She and her husband, Jim, reside in Valparaiso, Indiana.

Marilyn Meberg weaves God's Word together with real-life experience to provide hope and encouragement to all who listen. Speaking each year to 350,000 women at the Women of Faith conferences, Marilyn is also the author of several books. Marilyn lives in Texas. She has two children and two grandchildren.

Helen Widger Middlebrooke and her husband, Michael, live on Guam with their nine children. A freelance columnist, her weekly column on family and faith appears in the *Pacific Sunday News*, Agana, Guam.

Anita Renfroe is a comic force to be reckoned with, blending a potent mix of sass, edge, and humor. The bestselling author of *The Purse-Driven Life*, she makes her home in suburban Atlanta with her husband, John, and semi-grown children, Calvin, Austin, and Elyse. To find out more, visit her Web site at www.anitarenfroe.com.

Ramona Richards is an award-winning author and editor living in Tennessee. Formerly the editor of *Ideals* magazine, Ramona has also edited children's books, fiction, nonfiction, study Bibles, and reference books for major Christian publishers. Her books include *Secrets of Confidence* and *A Murder Among Friends*.

Toni Sortor is a freelance writer and editor in suburban New York. She has cowritten several Barbour books, including *The Word on Life*, *Prayers and Promises*, and *Daily Wisdom for Couples*.

Rachel St. John-Gilbert is an offbeat observer, who uses her wit to weave comic takes on the ordinary. Her writing has been called the "Seinfeld approach to daily devotions." Rachel lives in Texas with her husband and three children—a teenage son who's a ballkid for the Dallas Mavericks, and two preschool daughters who are bawlkids at home.